To JOAN —

WITH THE MOSTEST

Brooke Usst

Sam Leavitt

Jimmie Johnson

Hope Bryce

To Joan

to Joan —

George C Scott

Joanie —

Τίς ίδν ωλθην
Τὰυ συγγενέσθαι

Tom Ryan

Hi Joan —
Orson Bean

To Joan
Good Luck
Billy Strayhorn

To Joan with
best wishes and
thanks for the
charming hospitality
Otto *[illegible]*

Dear Joan —
Thank you for being
so nice to us
Jimmy Stewart.

To Joan
— thank you for the get
Well card + all the nice things
you did for us while we were
here
Arthur O'Connell

For sweet Joanie and
Bill, with warm best
wishes.   Robert Traver
            (John Voelker)

ANATOMY OF "ANATOMY"
The Making of a Movie

by
Joan G. Hansen

Layout design and ebook creation by Stacey Willey
Globe Printing, Inc., Ishpeming, MI
www.globeprinting.net

ISBN-13: 978-1493665266
2nd Edition 2013
ebook 2013

Author, Joan Hansen, 1950's

Preface

In 1958, St. Martin's Press of New York published a book entitled ANATOMY OF A MURDER, a novel written by John D. Voelker, a lawyer practicing in the small town of Ishpeming in the Upper Peninsula of Michigan. John Voelker wrote under the pen name Robert Traver, Robert being the name of his only son, who died in infancy, and Traver John's mother's maiden name.

A year later, in the spring of 1959, the novel was made into a movie which was directed by Otto Preminger and which starred James Stewart, Lee Remick, Ben Gazzara, and George C. Scott. The cast was also dotted with other well-known actors and actresses including Arthur O'Connell, Eve Arden, Murray Hamilton, and many more. Duke Ellington composed the musical score and appeared in one of the scenes.

Ishpeming, the author's home town, and Marquette, the nearby county seat, were two of the main sites for the filming, and other local areas were also used. The entire picture was shot on location, the first time this had been done. Until then a few shots might be done on location, with most of the scenes filmed in a Hollywood studio.

"Anatomy of a Murder" is a movie that has endured throughout the many years since its filming. It is still seen on television regularly, and at times is shown in theaters.

This book is an account of some of the incidents which occurred during the making of that movie, and it is written with love and nostalgia.

Author, Joan Hansen, 2013

Introduction

It was summer. It was 1952. The little town of Ishpeming in the Upper Peninsula of Michigan was quiet and peaceful then, and, for the most part, serene. With the small exception of an occasional minor upheaval, our Ishpeming slid through the days without even slightly furrowing its brow.

The winters, cold and snow-laden though they were, gave us skiing, skating parties, warm bowling alleys with cool beers, and the highlight of the year, our annual ski–jumping tournament.

When summer finally smiled on us once more, young women set aside their rolled-up jeans and donned dainty crinoline-lined party dresses which reached to their mid-calves, white gloves, and sometimes hats -- small, quiet statements or the large, floppy garden styles -- and wheeled their baby carriages, alone or in twos or threes, through the few blocks of "downtown." The playground became a medley of squeals, shouts, and the ringing notes of the Blue Notes Drum and Bugle Corps as it rehearsed for the next competition, which it invariably won. Open bedroom windows let in the click-clickety-click of the ladies' high heels and the songs of the robins and the long wails of the trains and the smell of the lilacs.

Nothing much ruffled us then. We took everything in our stride, even a murder in a nearby town. It was a curiosity, yes, and something to talk about in the yards and in the stores. But it was nothing that could change our coolly quiet patterns. That murder, though, did change us. We learned about best-sellers and how a movie is made. We met famous people who, but for that murder, would never have known that Ishpeming existed. Some of us would even become "movie stars" in minor ways. Yes, that murder stirred us up. But only for a while.

Contents

West Barnum Street 11

Getting Ready 21

The Mather Inn 26

Otto Preminger. 30

James Stewart and Arthur O'Connell 36

Murray Hamilton 42

Kathryn Grant 43

Duke Ellington 50

Eve Arden, Brooks West and the Welches. . 58

George C. Scott 60

Ben Gazzara. 63

Lee Remick 65

David and Patricia Silver. 68

Mount Shasta 72

The Crash 74

Lawrence Paquin 76

Cut! Prrrint! 79

West Barnum Street

John D. Voelker wrote the book ANATOMY OF A MURDER, a story which was based on that murder, under his pen name, Robert Traver.

John had called 205 West Barnum Street in Ishpeming, Michigan, his home for the greater part of his life. Not only was he raised there, but he and his wife Grace brought up their three daughters in that same family home. Even when he and Grace later built a beautiful house in the country, John still spoke often of his beloved Barnum Street, reminiscing about its gracious charm and its multitude of idiosyncrasies. When we would meet in later years at the post office or in a grocery store he would invariably call out, "Hi, Joanie! How's Barnum Street?"

Elizabeth "Honey-Bee" Voelker, John's oldest daughter, and I were very close friends during our high school years in the Upper Peninsula of Michigan in the late nineteen-forties. We lived one block apart, often walked to school together, and once sat on her back steps and bleached our almost-black bangs blond. It didn't work, they turned orange. Honey-Bee's mother was not amused. Neither were my two aunts, "the McCarthy girls of Barnum Street," who had raised me since my mother's death when I was five.

Honey-Bee and I wore each other's clothes, hung around Aunty's Restaurant, the gathering place of Ishpeming's youth, and I was even invited to accompany Grace and the girls to visit Grace's family on a Lower Michigan lake. Mainly though, we got in her father's hair when he was trying to listen to his records and we were in the living room giggling about boys.

At that time John Voelker was the Prosecuting Attorney of the County of Marquette in the central Upper Peninsula. He was also a much-published author of books and magazine articles. Two of his earlier books were concerned with his years as Marquette County Prosecutor, SMALL TOWN D.A. and TROUBLESHOOTER. Tales of some of the more colorful characters of our area, DANNY AND THE BOYS was a favorite of local residents. Later he was to pen his most famous piece, ANATOMY OF A MURDER, which occupied space on the best seller list for several months, and which was eventually made into a movie that has become a classic and is still shown regularly on television, and occasionally in movie theaters.

John was a handsome man resembling John Wayne, and he was always pleased when someone told him that. Music was his avocation. He loved to sit at the piano and chord to wandering melodies in an almost aimless, though relaxed and pleasant, style.

The son of a bar owner, John was always "Johnny" to the neighbors. He was born in the house on Barnum Street and the residents had known him since his infancy. Though he had grown up, become a lawyer and a writer and a prosecutor, and eventually even a Justice of the Michigan Supreme Court, this didn't matter. He was still just the kid down the block.

He used to like to tell me of his crush on the younger of my two aunts, Etta, whom the family called "Autie."

Autie was always beautiful, even in her later years. She possessed a dainty old-world grace and charm which once prompted a visitor from France to remark that she "looks like an old picture." Though we knew very well what he had meant by the statement we couldn't resist a bit of teasing, which she took with her usual vague smile. The man was right, though. Autie evoked visions of the portraits of calm, gentle ladies of days gone by.

She worked as a telephone operator at the Michigan Bell Telephone Company office located on the second floor of a building on the corner of Main and Division Streets. This was before technology had caught up with us, and we still picked up the phone and heard, "Number, please?" Autie worked the afternoon shift, and when it ended at eleven o'clock she would walk the few blocks to our house, passing the Voelker home. Little did she know that on some of these evenings

John and one of his buddies would duck behind the bushes just to watch her go by because she was so pretty. Of course this was just a school-boy crush as Autie was several years older than John, but he always loved to tell me about it.

Autie remained attractive and meticulously groomed until she went into the hospital for the last time at the age of eighty-six. No one was about to see her with her hair not washed and wound up into a perky little bun, or her clothes not neat and pressed. In her last years, after my other aunt, Flossie, had died, I would try to help her with some things, but nothing doing. My aunts helped others. You did not help them. Autie did agree to let me drive her to the grocery store during our treacherous, icy winter months, but as soon as the streets cleared in the spring she would trot out her wheeled grocery cart, a gift from one of two other cousins they had raised, and slowly make her way down Barnum to "Library Hill" and on to Joseph's Market on Cleveland Avenue.

While she was in the hospital that final time my husband and I bought her a copy of John's latest book, PEOPLE VERSUS KIRK, and John wrote in it, "To my old friend and neighbor, Etta McCarthy, from Joanie and Walter, with love, along with loads of luck and affection from the author. John Voelker (Robert Traver) November 1981."

Autie died just a few days after we gave her the book, and when I saw John in the grocery store the day after her death he wouldn't speak to me, just turned the other way. John always spoke to me when we met, often with a hug, but this was too much. He was having too hard a time handling the death of his old and dear friend from Barnum Street.

My aunts were always avid readers, devouring almost everything available in the Carnegie Public Library just two blocks away on the corner of Barnum and Main. When Anatomy was first out, they, of course, read it as soon as their names reached the top of its reserve list at the library. You should have heard the huffing and puffing!

"That Johnny Voelker, hmph!"

"Parnell *McCarthy*, is it? Hmph!"

To my old friend and neighbor, Etta McCarthy, from Joanie and Walter, with love, along with loads of luck and affection from the author.

John Voelker
(Robert Traver)

November 1981

It hit too close to home, this character Parnell McCarthy, drunken lawyer. We didn't have any lawyers in the McCarthy family but we sure had a few male members who enjoyed their nips, not excluding my dad. He was a Gallagher, yes, but he had been married to a McCarthy, and this made him part of the family.

But when the novel stayed and stayed on the best-seller list, and when the town started to experience the celebrity of having a movie made in its midst, the aunts, grudgingly at first, began to accept having their name attached to a guy who was "subject to the drink."

Eventually defeated in the election for Prosecutor by another Ishpeming lawyer, Edmund Thomas, John returned to the practice of law and continued to write. All of his many books were written at the same desk, which is now included in an exhibit called "The Voelker Room" at Northern Michigan University in Marquette.

For a time John served as a Justice of the Supreme Court of Michigan, and incidentally my second husband, Walter Hansen, then a young and budding lawyer, was chosen by John to be his law clerk. While filling this position Walter wrote an opinion entitled "Spence vs. Three Rivers" stating that it was not necessary to have "privity of contract" in order to sue a negligent manufacturer. Previously only the dealer could be sued in these instances, not the manufacturer. When we would meet, John would often bring this up and congratulate Walter on his expertise, a nice pat on the back for a lawyer. In later years he often said to Walter, "You and I should have practiced together." Walter would smile at this -- John a dyed-in-the wool Democrat and Walter a two-term Republican county chairman and loyal party worker. But they would have worked it out. Their friendship and respect for each other would have transcended any party lines. And they could have had some stirring arguments!

John considered Walter his personal lawyer. Once, many years ago, he walked into my husband's office and plunked a bottle of ale down on the desk. Walter picked it up and curiously examined it. There on the label was John Voelker's face.

"What's this all about?" Walter asked.

John smiled his slow and deliberate smile and leaned back comfortably in the big chair, as always in no hurry to dispense with the subject at hand. "Counselor," he began, "I 'll be damned if I know."

The story dated back to an event which had taken place while John was indulging in one of his favorite pastimes, playing cribbage at the Wonder Bar on Pearl Street, just off Main. A man came into the bar carrying artist supplies and asked John if he would mind if he sketched him. John murmured, "No, go ahead," and returned to the game, thinking the matter had ended there.

Some time later a friend mentioned to John that he had seen his picture on bottles of ale at White's Party Store in Marquette. Unable to figure this out, and having long since forgotten about the sketching in the Wonder Bar, John set out for Marquette only to see, much to his astonishment, his likeness beaming out from a bottle of Two-Hearted Ale. Not only did he find his picture, but also gracing the bottle was a direct quote from one of his pieces, "Testament of a Fisherman."

Seeing a bit pink, or perhaps bright red, John hightailed it to Walter's office.

"And here it is, Counselor. Exhibit A," he announced. "Do the necessary,"

Walter wrote a letter to the president of the Kalamazoo Brewing Company and received a very apologetic reply stating that it was all a misunderstanding, that he had been assured his company had been given permission to use John's face and words, and that he would be happy to pay any necessary royalties, this probably being prompted by the fact that the company had already distributed twelve thousand cases of the brew. Walter called John. "I'll be right over, Walter."

Again reclining in the big armchair across the desk from Walter, John stated, "Well, Walter, if I accept royalties in this matter, that will mean I'm in the beer business, and I have no desire to be in the beer business, even though my father was. I take it you'll send the appropriate missive in that regard. Just tell them to remove my pan and my quote from their damned bottle and I'll let it go at that."

Walter agreed, and John stood up and started to leave. Then he turned back to Walter. "Oh, by the way, Counselor, I believe you did agree to take this weighty matter on a contingency basis, isn't that right?"

Hiding a smile, Walter held out his hand. "I believe I did, Your Honor."

As he reached out to accept Walter's hand, the twinkle in John's eyes spread to his mouth, and they both indulged in a hearty laugh.

For many years that bottle of Two-Hearted Ale rested on a shelf behind my husband's desk in his office above the Peninsula Bank, and it now graces my treasured Voelker collection.

John's wife Grace was one of the loveliest people I've known. A beautiful woman with short dark hair and gently smiling eyes, her quiet movements and soft voice lent an aura of peace to their home, where friends were always welcome. She had time and a kind word for all of us, though we must have been babbling nuisances. The Voelker home was a gathering place for Honey-Bee's friends and, of course, for the friends of the two younger daughters, Julie and Gracie. I think there were times when John wished it were less of a gathering place so he could enjoy a little peace and quiet, but those thoughts were never put into words as far as I know. For the most part he just seemed to ignore all the commotion. I suspect he chose to pretend we weren't there.

Except for me.

I was Barnum Street. I was his old friends' niece. I was as big a bottom-pain as any of the others, but that didn't matter. I was accepted. There was always a "High, Joanie!" for me.

The Voelker house was large and handsome. Standing on a big corner lot where Barnum meets Pine Street, the building was adorned with an open porch on two sides and surrounded by lush greens and bushes and trees. In the back yard stood a real, stand-up-inside play-house, every little girl's dream. Since Honey-Bee and I didn't become close friends until I had graduated from St. John's Catholic School and had entered high school, I never played mommy or had tea parties in that playhouse, a fact which always held a touch of disappointment for me. When I became a bit of a fixture in the Voelker home, the dolls and furniture and tea set within the little house had grown dusty and forgotten.

West Barnum Street was only three blocks long, short small-town blocks. It was a lovely street, resting quietly above the cavernous Cliffs Shaft underground mine, now closed, which stretched under most of Ishpeming. We all set our clocks by the twice daily tremors evoked at blasting time, at seven in the morning and three in the af-ternoon. Sometimes a picture would work its way off the wall, or a glass would slip off a table. We school kids loved the afternoon blast because it meant that the day's session was almost over and we would soon be free. The shaft itself and the railroad yard were just a half block west of my aunts' house, and the switching ore cars sang to us day and night. We didn't mind. It was just part of Ishpeming and Barnum Street.

In summer the leaves of the trees would meet in the center of our street, making eery green and yellowish shadows which danced over the cracked and heaved sidewalks on which the long, hard win-ters had taken their toll. During those winters we walked in the road, hugging the high snowbanks to avoid the cars, as the sidewalks were not plowed. My one aunt, though, Flossie, didn't hug any banks. She walked right down the middle of the road expecting the cars to avoid *her*. And they did. Everybody knew my aunts.

It was a very Irish street. Besides my McCarthy family there were Harringtons, Flynns, Gleasons, Kennedys, Hugheses and Nolans. All his life when we'd meet on the street or in one of the grocery stores, John would speak to me of our Barnum street with love and pride. It was always his darlin' home, even after he and Grace moved to their new location. I have several notes he wrote to me over the years, many of them making some mention of his cherished first home. Once I sent him a tape of Irish songs which I had sung and accompanied on the piano at the request of all my cousins, and he wrote, "As soon as I can get my player fixed we'll play your tape. We'll look forward to the prospect and meanwhile thank you for remembering these old inhabitants of Irish Lane: old West Barnum Street, a place that used to read like a map of Dublin, begorrah!"

Most lots on West Barnum were deep and narrow, and thus the houses were built with that configuration. A common design would greet us with a front hall which held the stairway to the second floor and which opened into both the parlor and, down a hall, into the living room. Side by side with the living room would be a den or library. In the house I lived in this library area was used as a bedroom and was separated from the living room by French doors. At the Voelkers' however, this room, which served as John's inner sanctum, was made distinct from its neighbor only by an open archway. Next in line, behind the living room and den, would be the dining room, and finally the kitchen, usually with a walk-in pantry. The bedrooms, or at least most of them, could be found on the second floor. The Voelker house followed this pattern, as did my aunts'.

Everything was old and welcoming inside the Voelker home, from the parlor to the long narrow pantry in back. The living room and den next to it serve as John's office in the movie made from his book. At the Voelkers' the phone was in the pantry, which I thought was wonderful. Ours was in the then-traditional spot, proudly displayed on a table in the living room. But the pantry! It seemed so exotic to the teen-ager I was.

In our house the telephone was a major part of our existence. Both of my aunts were telephone operators, Flossie for The Cleveland-Cliffs Iron Company and Autie for The Michigan Bell Telephone Company, known better as Michigan Bell. Flossie sat in a large office on the second floor of one of the two sprawling Cliffs office buildings, plugging cords into and out of the wooden PBX desk. Autie's was one of the voices we heard when we picked up the phone to make a call. "Number, please?" When our phone rang in a certain way, one or the other of them would say, "That's long distance." And she'd be right. I never could figure out how they knew. But they did.

Unfortunately for John, our favorite spot to sit was the living room, right next to his den. The room was small, with soft, comfortable old furniture, and was warmed by a welcoming Ben Franklin iron stove which stood in one corner. This room and John's room next to it are the rooms in which the office scenes of the movie were filmed.

During the filming there came a need for an old stove-top coffee pot to be used in the office scenes. It couldn't be new and shiny, but rather must have the marks of age and loving use. My aunts had just the pot. I borrowed it for the movie company and it became a focal spot for some of the office episodes, often carried by Eve Arden. I wish I knew what happened to it after it was returned to me. Quite likely one of the cousins gave my aunts a fancy new electric percolator one Christmas and those dear ladies threw their movie star away. A shame.

In that den John had all his musical equipment, very sophisticated for those days, and here he spent long evening hours listening to his beloved record collection. One of his favorite songs was "As Time Goes By" from Casablanca. Fortunately in our teenage days John had earphones, quite new at the time, as we chattering girls and sometimes a few boys would often be sprawled around the next room.

From this den James Stewart places a phone call to Lee Remick in the movie, giving his phone number as 700. Ours was then 300. Dial telephones hadn't reached us at the time of the murder, as everything of that nature was very slow to get to the Upper Peninsula. We didn't even get touch-tone until 1994 in some parts of our area. John loved it that way. After the Mackinac bridge was built and the ferry boats between the upper and lower peninsulas became things of the past, John often jokingly declared that he was going to blow up the bridge and keep all those Detroiters out of our fair U.P.

I graduated from high school in 1950 and went off to Marquette University in Milwaukee to study journalism, returning home after two years to marry Bill Lehmann, a young man I had dated while in high school. Honey-Bee graduated two years after I did, the year I was married.

In the summer of 1952, Bill and I were sitting in one of the beautiful old high-backed wooden booths in Aunty's, still the watering hole and social hub of the younger people, married or single. We were just about to insert a nickel into the tiny juke box on the wall of our booth in order to play one of the songs of 1952 when suddenly the door opened and in rushed Honey-Bee, looking very wide-eyed. Spotting us, she came quickly over to our booth and sat down next to me, announcing as she did, "There's been a murder!" Her beautiful big eyes opened even wider, and she looked more like her mother than ever.

"A murder?" we both asked, astonished. Other things besides dial telephones had not as yet reached the Upper Peninsula, and crime was, at least partially, among them. Shocks such as this one were few and far between. The quiet and sheltered life we enjoyed in our lovely peninsula was attributable, at least in part, to our separation from the rest of the state by the Straits of Mackinac, and from Canada by Lake Superior. Not many outside influences wormed their way into our tranquil existence.

"In Big Bay," Bee went on. "At the local bar." Honey-Bee had a summer job that year at Bay Cliff, a camp for special needs children that was located in that small town on Lake Superior just a few miles northwest of Marquette.

"Who was murdered?" Bill queried.

"The bar owner. I don't know his name. Some man just walked in, headed for the bar, and shot him."

"Does anyone have an idea why?" I wondered, enjoying the prospect of having something so exciting to talk about. Honey-Bee had our undivided attention.

"No one seems to know much about it yet," she told us. "They're still investigating."

That night and that story were to mean much more to all of us than we could possibly have known as we talked that summer evening. The shooting in Big Bay gave us ANATOMY OF A MURDER, the book, and "Anatomy of a Murder," the movie. John would write the book, many of us would participate in the movie, and our little town would be jump-started with the electrical charge of a major motion picture being filmed in our midst. We would brush elbows with famous actors, actresses, directors, musicians, cameramen, costume designers, and sound engineers.

Bill and I heard the story from Elizabeth Voelker, daughter of John D. Voelker, who would put the essence of that murder into a best-selling novel. None of us could have known, then, just what it portended for us all.

Getting Ready

Henry Weinberger and Boris Leven came to Ishpeming on a cold, windy day in January and stayed at the Mather Inn, where I was working as the dining room hostess. Henry Weinberger was to serve as production manager of "Anatomy of a Murder," and Boris Leven would be its art director. Mr. Weinberger was a big, somewhat gruff man, while Mr. Leven offered a contrasting small frame and slightly accented, quiet voice. They were in Ishpeming to scout the county for places in which to film the scenes. It was 1959.

The past year had not been a good one for our area. Highly dependent on the iron mining industry, it suffered greatly when the companies began to cut back and to lay off hundreds of workers. Unemployment compensation was running out for many, and families were scared. What would they do?

My husband, Bill Lehmann, was one of those laid off, and we had decided that he would return to school at nearby Northern Michigan University in Marquette, our county seat. During that period we both worked at many jobs in order to keep our house and support our two sons. I had started as a clerk in Johnson's Drug Store, and then the Mather Inn hostess, who had been in that position for many years, decided to retire. I applied for the job and got it.

I worked three shifts -- breakfast, lunch and dinner every day but Friday, going home in between shifts to attempt to keep up on the housework and cooking. Karl, our older boy, was in kindergarten at the time, and Kurt was three. At those ages they can mess up a lot of clothes. And they do have to eat. We weren't dependent on fast foods in those days, and even if they had existed not many could afford to purchase them.

Mr. Weinberger and Mr. Leven traveled all over Marquette County, driven by a local man who was out of work. Hopes had been high that the movie would provide jobs. One driver was a start. There would be more jobs to follow, we were all sure.

The stately old Marquette County courthouse was, of course, the logical choice for the courtroom scenes. Located in the city of Marquette, about sixteen miles from Ishpeming, this grand old lady was built in 1902. She occupies a full block on the side of a hill and is graced with lovely grounds. There are entrances on three sides, each approached by cement steps and boasting large columns at the entrance doors. The main entrance stands far back from the street and is gained access by climbing first one short flight of steps, then proceeding along a wide sidewalk, and finally by climbing a second, much longer, flight. It takes a lot of puff to get into that building!

Outside there is one instance where only Mr. Welch, nattily dressed and with a flower in his lapel, walks down the street, passes the jail, and proceeds up those steps and into the courthouse

Inside are more steps, these of softly gleaming Italian marble, with the main center stairway branching out into narrower ones on each side. Stars and extras would often be shown scurrying up those lovely stairs.

There are two courtrooms, one smaller than the other. The major courtroom, in which the filming took place, is grand with its wood, its columned balconies, and its huge stained glass dome. The judge's bench and the walls and door behind it are all hand-carved cherry, some of the railings are stained oak, and the benches are of maple with hand-carved armrests at each end. Portraits of past judges hang on the walls.

The jail scenes were filmed in and around the Marquette County jail which is located next to the courthouse, with a hall as access between the two buildings. Marquette County has a large Finnish population, accounting for Jimmy Stewart's speaking to the jailer as Sulo, and a bartender in an earlier scene bearing the name Toivo, both Finnish names quite common in this area.

Work began. The old girl was transformed. Heavy scaffolding and supports had to be erected over the stairway in order to transport all the weighty filming equipment to the main courtroom on the second floor, and to keep the courtroom floor from ending up in the basement. Lighting gear occupied many areas of the room. Directors' chairs hid behind cameras. When the filming finally commenced, judges and lawyers had to use alternative rooms for their trials. This part of the filming lasted about six weeks.

Always fun for us locals to watch is the opening scene in which James Stewart drives into Ishpeming and turns at the Peninsula Bank building onto Main Street. According to today's rules, he's going the wrong way on a one-way street, but it wasn't a one-way street in 1959. We didn't have, or need, any. There wasn't that much traffic. Also those garish street lights which most of us hated when they were installed have now been replaced.

Jimmy passes some buildings which still exist, though with minor alterations, and some others which have disappeared over the years. One of the survivors is the Peninsula Bank, on the second floor of which was located my husband's law offices, which also are now gone. We see Old Ish, the statue of an Indian which has stood guard over our downtown area for as long as most of us can remember. Before sanitation became so important, Old Ish had several bubbling drinking fountains and troughs for dogs and horses which held the expected blend of water, leaves, sand and whatever else nature and the animals could deposit within. The fountains and troughs are now also just a memory. My aunts were fussy about such things and had forbidden me to drink from the fountains which, predictably, led me seldom to pass without at least a sip. Unless, of course, I was accompanied by one or both of those ladies.

In this opening scene, Paul Biegler, a thinly disguised John Voelker, is coming home from a day of fly fishing, a favorite pastime of John as well, a pastime which brought us "Anatomy of a Fisherman", "Trout Madness", "Testament of a Fisherman," and other pieces. Every once in a while John would drop over to our house with a mouth-watering mess of brook trout. Lucky us.

The bar in Big Bay where the murder took place was used as just that in the movie -- the scene of the murder. Behind the bar could still be found the hole where the perpetrator's bullet had entered the wall. An addition was constructed on an old hotel, then called the Big Bay Inn, to represent the outside of the bar. It was just a shell, but was later finished by the owners and is still in use, now under the movie name, Thunder Bay Inn. When one of the actors went through a door in the hotel and then was seen entering the bar, he or she had actually walked down the street to the place where the bar scenes would be filmed.

Also taking place in Big Bay was Arthur O'Connell's car crash.

Mount Shasta Lodge, a restaurant and lounge in the nearby town of Michigamme, was chosen for one scene. "Shasta" is a log building which was moved to that site on highway U.S. 41 just east of the town of Michigamme in 1939 by Maurice and Norma Ball, who still owned it during the making of the movie. It was later purchased by their son and daughter-in-law, Bob and Stella Ball, and since then has changed hands several times. Situated across from beautiful Lake Michigamme, a large lake with many islands and bays, Shasta looks out over that lake and the park and its pavillion. Part of the filming would take place inside the restaurant and part in the parking lot.

The lovely old Carnegie Public Library in Ishpeming became the law library where James Stewart and Arthur O'Connell do their research. On a corner at the top of a steep hill, it has a half-circle of cement steps leading up from the corner itself rather than being on either Main or Barnum. Instead, the stairs are on both streets. As we walk in the door, laboriously catching our breath, we face the old wooden librarian's desk, behind which I often stood while in high school. The wage then was fifty cents an evening. In the reading room to the left we find large tables built of solid, heavy wood polished to gleaming mirrors with years of fond attention. Their accompanying chairs are comfortable and inviting. Here the older gentlemen of the town have spread out their newspapers since the day the library opened, and here also the lonely ones have found quiet companionship. In past days this room also held several sets of reference books, and grade school and high school students would pour over piles of encyclopedias and hurriedly scratch pages of notes. Unfortunately, though, computers are beginning to rob our youth of this quiet, tranquil method of research.

To the right of the main desk is another vast, book-lined area also boasting shiny wood tables and chairs, and the area directly behind the desk is the reference room. This area is looked down upon from a balcony which has a translucent glass floor. As a child I was always afraid the glass would break and I would go sailing to the floor below. I still have a bit of anxiety when I walk up there, but try to behave like an adult. Following the curve of the balcony the shelves spray out like spokes of a wheel. Jimmy Stewart would be seen leaning over that railing and talking to Arthur O'Connell below.

Ishpeming's railroad depot, now gone, was chosen for, what else, the railroad shots.

Little by little the plans fell into place.

Applications were taken for many types of jobs. Hope was returning. The company, Carlyle Productions, a subsidiary of Columbia Pictures, hired drivers to transport actors and staff in its large fleet of cars to the various filming sites. Max Slater, assistant to the producer, aided by his wife Margo, signed up extras to play townspeople, courtroom spectators, jurors and others. The extras made $10.00 per day, not much by today's standards but a godsend to those in need at the time. A dollar went much further in those days.

Weinberger and Leven left for California. They would return in the spring and the filming would begin.

The Mather Inn

Built, and owned for many years, by The Cleveland-Cliffs Iron Company as a convenience for their visiting executives and sales people, the Mather Inn was a charming large colonial-style brick building standing majestically on a full Ishpeming block at the edge of the downtown district. It was named after William G. Mather, a company executive who also had one ore boat of the Cliffs fleet named in his honor, aboard which I was once privileged to take a trip. That ore carrier later became a museum in Cleveland.

Approaching the open porch and entrance to the lobby is a long sidewalk followed by a flight of wide cement steps. In the summer during those long-ago years, the entire sprawling front yard was a collage of green grass edged with flowers of many colors and varieties, and it offered a perfect setting for the weekly Ishpeming City Band concerts. Snowtime was Winter Carnival time, with many of the events taking place on the Mather Inn grounds during the February festivities. A queen would be chosen from the many young women who were asked to vie for it, and those not elected queen would provide her escort. Many hands would toil together over the beautiful throne of ice from which the queen would survey her subjects after her coronation. Luckily the queen's robe was made of quite heavy velvet, under which she could wear snow gear. Otherwise that throne would have loomed mighty cold, and there probably would not have been very many candidates for the royal honor.

After the coronation, the queen and her court would go on to reign over the annual ski-jumping tournament at Ishpeming's Suicide Hill, one of the oldest jumping hills in the country. That tournament still takes place each year in late February.

The tournament was one of the highlights of our year and drew jumpers from all over the world. Locals and visitors swarmed to the scene, going early to get good parking spots so that they could escape the cold in their warm cars. During World War II when gas was scarce and rationed, many of us would walk out to the hill. Usually some kind soul, lucky enough to own a car and to have a bit of gas, would stop and let us cram ourselves into his or her car. Much of the time we didn't even know each other. In those days in our U.P., as we fondly call the Upper Peninsula, many families didn't even own cars. If we couldn't afford something, we did without it, something almost unheard of today.

A tradition meant only for the young and vigorous consisted of climbing up to the end of the wooden take-off to watch the riders as they flew by, almost close enough to touch. In those days before the advent of aerodynamics, the jumpers wore baggy ski pants which whirred in the breeze and which produced a thrilling sound as they sailed past the spectators lining the top of the hill. Now, of course, the pants are almost skin tight.

And the length of each jump did not appear miraculously on some type of computer. There were markers, very warmly dressed men of all ages who lined the hill from the take-off to the flat ground, and one of those in the vicinity of the spot at which the rider touched ground would place the tip of his long wooden pointer down at that exact spot.

* * *

In the large lobby of The Mather Inn were found big, high-backed leather chairs, smaller ones covered with tapestry and other lovely materials, warm, rich wood tables, and a mahogany front desk. On cold winter nights the fireplace was always crackling and twinkling, sending dancing shadows throughout the room as guests and towns-folk sipped or visited.

Down a short hall to the west was the Elliott Room, named after S. R. Elliott, one of the early managers of the Ishpeming-area operations of the Cleveland-based iron mining company. Warmed by its wood walls, this room contained a long mahogany meeting or dining table lined with armchairs. The front wall of the Elliott Room consisted entirely of windows and window seats which offered a view of the gardens, a pleasant place to sit and visit or enjoy a cocktail or a cup of tea. Not a large room, it was used primarily for meetings, bridge luncheons, wedding rehearsal dinners and the like.

Across from the Elliott Room, on the north side of the building and somewhat larger than the Elliott Room, was the Swiss Room. A short railed stairway led down to the main area, which was decorated with posters from all over the world. I suppose there were more from Switzerland than other places, hence the name. Lunch or dinner was served here when the main dining room was occupied with parties, the Rotary Club, or other large functions. A popular setting for private gatherings, the Swiss Room could accommodate larger social or business groups than its counterpart across the hall.

At the end of this hall was a small suite which was occasionally used for meetings, card parties, or cocktail entertaining. This became the suite in which Jimmy Stewart resided during his stay in Ishpeming.

And then, reigning royally over the building and the grounds and occupying the entire east end of the structure we found the main dining room. Bright and sunny, its curved-top windows lighting three sides, the Georgian Room was a welcoming, enfolding haven in which to dine, sip cocktails, and sometimes dance. Under the expert guidance of chef Howard Schrandt, dining at the Mather Inn was very special. Its Sunday buffet was sumptuous and included lobster Newburg, and bore the unbelievably low cost of $2.98. I have always had a special spot in my heart for lobster Newburg, and Howard would set aside a bowl of it for me each Sunday. I'm not so sure the manager would have approved, but I was in heaven.

During the week a full menu was served, with the Mather Inn undoubtedly being one of the last restaurants still following the practice of having the customer write out his or her order. There were many times when I pitied those in the kitchen trying to decipher the scratching.

The Georgian Room was the favorite spot of local people for cocktail parties too large for the Swiss or Elliott rooms, and it could accommodate dancing if this was desired. During the ski tournament the Snow Ball was held here, with a full orchestra guiding the elegantly dressed ladies and gentlemen around the dance floor, giving the room an extra bit of sparkle.

From the coatroom just outside the entrance to the Georgian Room led a stairway which took us down to the Tap Room, another inviting and cozy place to sip. Graced with wood booths and leather sofas and chairs, it was a much-chosen place for locals or guests to meet. This bar was also a noisy, bustling spot during the ski-jumping tournament. Spectators and jumpers alike gathered here to swap stories and compare the day's rides. Distance and form, distance and form! Those words floated throughout the room. Congratulations abounded for the fortunate ones who had met, or even exceeded, their goals, and some teasing or condolences were directed toward those who were not so lucky. With riders present from all over the world, the air was rich with many tongues.

On the second floor overlooking the grounds another gracious touch had been added -- the ladies' lounge next door to one of the ladies' restrooms. Entered through French doors and lined with comfortable pastel sofas and chairs, it was a spot in which to rest and visit, a site for card parties and, during large functions, a coat checkroom. The back entrance to the hotel was across from this room, as the Mather Inn is built into one of Ishpeming's many hills, necessitating that the rear access be on the second level. This part of the building is on the one block of East Barnum Street.

And those were the primary sites. The rest was up to the directors, actors and crew.

What was to evolve would become a classic.

Otto Preminger

On his first evening in Ishpeming, Otto Preminger, producer and director of the film, strode into the dining room followed by an entourage of the company staff, all strangers to me that evening but soon to become familiar names and faces. Looking very stern and important, and casting a much larger shadow than his medium-sized frame would warrant, it was obvious that Mr. Preminger was aware that all eyes were on him. He looked directly at no one and appeared oblivious to his audience.

Surveying the surroundings with cold blue eyes, he had the aura of a lion about to pounce on his latest prey -- that prey being Ishpeming, a town not as yet conquered, and "Anatomy of a Murder," a movie not as yet made. Reveling in the attention, though still giving the impression of not noticing it, he took a seat at the large table that had been prepared for him, and his companions followed suit. The waitresses and I all shook. We had heard and read the many tales of his temper, his rudeness, his bullying of others. I approached that table with much trepidation.

As it turned out, we never felt those stings. He was always polite, though demanded perfection, and I found, having later been invited to watch the filming whenever I could find the time, that he treated his actors with respect and courtesy. Once, though, he lost his temper when a grip dropped a light fixture during what might have been a final take. He really laced into the poor guy.

Another person, a secretary, was good evidence of what the consequences would be if someone displeased Otto.

She lived at the Northland in Marquette but occasionally visited the

Inn for lunch or dinner. On one of these occasions she came into the dining room very drunk and proceeded to drink more and more. Suddenly she began to attack me verbally. I don't know what I ever did to cause her to be so venomous toward me. Nothing, as far as I could remember. I hardly knew her. The others told me later that she was prone to such outbreaks when something completely unrelated was distressing her, and especially when she had been drinking heavily.

She called across the room from the table where she was sitting with a small group, "Cashier! Cashier!" The term and the way it was shouted were decidedly deprecating, even without the snarl in her voice. I was known as a hostess, not a cashier, though if someone had called me cashier in a pleasant tone of voice it wouldn't have offended me at all.

Since I was busy showing some people to a table, I didn't respond immediately, and she began calling me again, becoming even louder and more rude. "I want to pay my bill. Don't you know what your job is? Get over here!"

The people at her table tried to persuade her to stop but their efforts just aggravated her into getting worse, so finally one of the men in her group removed her, almost bodily, from the dining room.

I never saw her again. When Mr. Preminger was told of it, he sent her packing.

Mr. Preminger also became quite annoyed with the morning cook at one time. John Voelker often brought him some of the tasty, succulent brook trout which he caught in the many streams he frequented. Otto wanted them fried in butter for his breakfasts, but the cook insisted on frying them in oil. Each day the director would politely ask that the next time they be cooked in butter. And each day, for whatever reason we'll never know, the breakfast cook would again use oil. Finally one day Otto came to me and said through clenched teeth, "Joanie, tell the cook if he fries those bee-uu-tee-ful fish in oil next time, he can eat them himself!" My husband, who loves brook trout, said, "If I were the chef I'd take him up on it -- hide the butter!"

I still hear accounts of Otto's terrorizing, though. Stars are often quoted in the press and on television even today, long after his death, giving details of their bad experiences while working with Preminger. But in almost three months of knowing him, seeing him at breakfast and dinner and on the sets, I certainly never encountered any of it. I suppose many of those stories were true. There are too many to have all been fabricated. But none will come from me, as I didn't experience anything but courtesy from him during those months.

As I passed around the menus that first evening, Mr. Preminger asked in a commanding voice, "Vat is your best vine?"

I told him, though after all these years I can't remember what it was.

He frowned a bit, but said, "I vill try it."

Trembling inside, I fetched the bottle from the wine storage room. (We couldn't really call it a cellar.) I knew this was going to be a disaster. I would break the cork. I'd drop the bottle in his lap. Or, horror of horrors, I would spill the whole thing all over his shining head.

But all went well. The cork came out fine and I poured the customary small amount of wine for him to taste. He sipped, wrinkled his nose slightly, looked none too happy, and asked, "This is the best you have?"

"Yes," I told him. I didn't know if it was the best or not. I just knew it was the most expensive.

"All right," he surrendered. "It vill be fine."

And as I filled his glass he looked up and smiled at me. Gone was the haughty look, his face and those cold blue eyes becoming almost gentle. I still trembled inside, but a bit less.

Friday was my day off, and since Mr. Preminger had told me that I was permitted to visit the courtroom set (spectators were barred), I tried to sneak in a few hours on some Fridays. Unfortunately I had to do my housework on Fridays, since there wasn't much time between the breakfast, lunch and dinner hours to accomplish a great deal, but I made time to watch at least some of the filming. Probably the house suffered, but I had fun.

The first time I went to the set I watched some of the testimony in the courtroom from a special seat they put behind the camera for me. Peeking around Sam Leavitt, the cinematographer, and his crew all afternoon, I learned with fascination how a scene was rehearsed and rehearsed, again and again, until Otto was satisfied. Then the takes began, once more repeated over and over until Otto saw perfection in one and called out in his Viennese accent, "Cut! Prrrint!"

When the day's shooting was drawing to an end on the first day I attended, Hal Polaire, assistant to the director, came to me with a questionnaire of sorts to fill out -- address, social security number, etc. It turned out that they were going to pay me as an extra! Mr. Preminger was a very generous man, though much maligned, as we all know.

Otto liked my two boys. Once in a while my husband would stop in with them so I could at least say hello, but we didn't make it a regular practice and they never stayed long. As a treat for me on Easter Sunday, since I had to work, Bill dressed Karl and Kurt in their little sportcoats and took them to the Inn for lunch. As Kurt was only three, the waitress brought us a high chair for him. Nothing doing. He was not about to sit in it. Kurt didn't yowl or whine, that wasn't his nature. But the ability to be stubborn *was* his nature, and nobody was going to get him into that chair. He just stood there, staring at the floor and not budging an inch. Finally we gave in and let him sit with his chin barely reaching the table's edge. Booster seats had not been invented yet, or if they had, the Mather Inn didn't possess any. The booster seats of the time were Sears Roebuck and "Monkey" Ward catalogs. Not telephone books, at least in not our area. Our phone books were only about a half inch thick. Of course my son ended up with a very colorful little sport coat to accompany him back home.

The boys received a lot of attention that day. Jimmy Stewart came to talk to them as did Eve Arden and many of the company. Kurt was a bit too young to realize how well-known some of them were, but Karl, at five, had seen James Stewart in one movie, and was thrilled to meet him.

Incidentally, Karl is now the retired manager of two hotels and Kurt is still a practicing pediatrician. The years do pass, don't they?

Tom Ryan, Mr. Preminger's reader, was impressed by how well-behaved they were.

"And they behaved like children," he enthused. "In L.A. most kids never really are children. They act like miniature adults. Grow up too soon."

It must be noted, however, that they were on their best behavior. Angels they were not.

Tom Ryan liked to joke about how he hated the Upper Peninsula and its weather. Actually, though he didn't know it, we were having a fairly nice spring, as our springs go.

One morning he came into the dining room with a big grin on his face and handed me a sheet of paper.

"I wrote this for you last night," he told me, still grinning. "It's to the tune of 'On the Street Where You Live.' "

On one side of the paper was a copy of the agreement which participants in the movie had to sign before they could begin work for Carlyle Productions. On the back was written, all in capital letters and with sporadic punctuation, and no, those aren't misprints:

I HAVE OFTEN WORKED ON A FILM BEFORE
BUT THE TEMPERATURE NEVER WENT TO MINUS 4.
HOW I WISH THAT SPRING
CAME TO ISHPEMING
OH I WANT TO GO BACK TO L.A.

PEOPLE STOP AND STARE HOW THEY BOTHER ME
THERE ARE FIFTY MILLION PLACES I WOULD RATHER BE
OTTO CALL "CUT! PRINT!"
AND THEN WATCH US SPRINT
OH I WANT TO GO BACK TO LA

AND ALL THOSE GODAWFUL LUNCHES
EVERY NOON IN DEAR OLD MARQUETTE
THOSE OVERPOWERING HUNCHES
THAT WE ARE SICK BECAUSE OF SOMETHING THAT WE ET.

HERE WE WORK 6 DAYS TO GET ONE DAY OFF
AND EACH ONE OF US HAS HAD
THE FLU OR WHOOPING COUGH
VOELKER DID HIS BEST
BUT THIS AINT THE WEST
OH I WANT TO GO BACK TO LA.

* * *

Hope Bryce, Mr. Preminger's fiancée and the costume coordinator for the film, was a former model, very tall and very thin and extremely beautiful. Soft-spoken and friendly, Hope was easy to know. She would glide up to my desk with the liquid walk of an experienced model, and we would chat and joke over many subjects

Her dinner was often soup and a tomato. Yes. That was all. Of course she had to maintain that svelte model's figure. Occasionally, though, she would be tempted by one of Howard's succulent presentations, and would splurge.

Then she would stop at my desk and moan, "Oh, Joanie, I've got to get back to those tomatoes!"

It must be remembered that these were the fifties and that this was the U.P., as we affectionately call our Upper Peninsula. Sleeping together while not married was, of course, done, even here, but it was not talked about. So Otto and Miss Bryce had separate rooms. Victorian, yes, and a waste of the company's money, because the maids all knew that only one room was being slept in. And they told. Oh, did they tell!

"Did you hear . . .?"

"No, tell us !"

"Well, I was going down the hall and . . ."

Muffled giggles. "Oh, my gosh!"

It was admirable of Otto, though, not to want to shock the pants off this staid and old-fashioned little town. Believe me, we had our diseases. But they were safely hidden under the rug.

Mr. Preminger and Miss Bryce later married and became the parents of twins.

James Stewart and Arthur O'Connell

After Mr. Preminger and the directors had descended on us, members of the cast began to arrive daily on the Chicago and Northwestern railroad -- James Stewart, Eve Arden, Lee Remick and a host of others. The big stars and higher echelon of staff stayed at the Mather Inn, while second and third assistant directors, grips, lighting people, secretaries and those with minor roles called the Northland Hotel in Marquette their home for the duration of the filming. The Northland was another grand old U.P. edifice and is now known as The Landmark Inn.

There was not much in the way of air travel up our way in the fifties, and train travel was wonderful. The trains came from Chicago, at one time pulled by coal-burning engines from which one disembarked feeling like a Welsh miner, but later the "streamliner" was introduced, causing quite a stir at first. About half of the town turned out at about two in the morning to greet "The 400" on its first run. Ishpeming was its last stop. From there it retreated to the "round house" for cleaning and inspection.

The Mather Inn bustled. Even with two dinner seatings each evening, reservations were a must, and the dining room was always full. People came from all over the U.P. and northern Wisconsin to peek at the stars from behind their forks and coffee cups while the cast visited with each other and tried to relax after the long days of shooting. Most of the guests were polite, though, and didn't interrupt the actors during their meals, but of course there are always a few who are rude. It was my job to head them off at the pass. I hated that part.

The company had breakfast and dinner in the dining room, with lunch being catered on the set by the Inn.

At about six or so each evening, depending on the shooting schedule and the length of the drive, the company cars would begin to pull up to the hotel's second-floor back door to discharge their passengers. The stars would disembark, perhaps sign a few autographs, and descend to the lobby by way of the stairs or in the small elevator which didn't always operate properly and was sometimes slower than taking the stairs. After stopping at the desk for keys and mail, they would head for their rooms.

It wasn't long, though, before the exodus to the Tap Room would begin. In ones, twos or groups they would troop down the stairs, through the lobby, and down one more flight to the bar, where Boris Leven would order his martini "five-to-one." Those were the days of the awful two gin to one vermouth martinis. Now it's "no vermouth," isn't it? Or perhaps a drop.

The company began work very early each morning, and when the day's efforts had been completed and wrapped up they were ready for fun. John Voelker, normally not one who enjoyed socializing in public places, was there most evenings, sometimes with Grace accompanying him. He would hold court from one of the sofas, telling fish stories as only John Voelker could tell them. The Tap Room was jumping. As was the Georgian Room.

Many scenes were played out in that room. Friendships were struck up, even romances, and some irritations developed. You can't put that many people together, day after day, evening after evening, without some problems. But they weren't major ones and were resolved quite readily. For the most part it was an atmosphere of friendly relaxation.

Jimmy Stewart had the suite at the end of the hall on the first floor. There he and Arthur O'Connell would play cards for a while and then come to the dining room for dinner, Jimmy strolling easily, his lanky, slender frame seeming to experience no effort with movement. Though Mr. O'Connell was much more serious, sometimes even dour, they both always had a cheery greeting and perhaps a bit of teasing for me.

Jimmy often asked, "What's good tonight, Joanie?" (The menu seldom changed except for the smaller accompaniments.)

I would close my eyes, point to something on one of the pages, and say, "This one is especially tasty." It was a simple little game, but it was our game and we had a bit of fun with it.

One night I led him and Arthur O'Connell to a table for two by a front window, placed their menus before them and started to walk away.

"Oh, Joanie," I heard in Jimmy's unmistakable voice. Could anyone miss that slow, slightly nasal intonation? I turned.

"Yes?"

He lifted his menu. It was only a cover. There was nothing inside. Pointing at a spot, he declared, "I'll have that one. It sounds awful good," and looked up at me with a straight, unsmiling face, but there was no mistaking the twinkle in those handsome eyes.

The waitresses were terrified of O'Connell, as he could growl if things were not to his liking. He enjoyed a beer with his dinner but wanted only about an inch poured into his glass. To the waitresses' amusement he wouldn't let anyone pour it but me. I guess, and I believe they too suspected, that they could have accomplished that great feat just as well as I.

But if Mr. O'Connell's needs were adequately met, he was very nice. Quietly spoken, he was a courteous gentleman, not given to smiling a lot, but at least minus the growl. If his needs were met.

Mr. O'Connell developed pneumonia during the filming and had to be sent to Francis A. Bell Memorial Hospital in Ishpeming. He cursed our climate and blamed it for his malady. Though the filming was done in what should have been spring, our springs can be worse than the winters in most places. We get some of our most ferocious snowstorms in March and even April, and the cold weather hangs on and on.

"It's this damned rotten weather of yours, Joanie," he would say as he coughed and sneezed and suffered with his "cold."

"I didn't order it, Mr. O'Connell," would be my answer.

He didn't notify his friends at home of his hospitalization until later, and I cemented our budding friendship by sending him the only get-well card he received. And my being all Irish didn't hurt either, with a guy named O'Connell.

At the time of the filming of Anatomy, Arthur had never been married. As my dear husband loved to say, "He never made the same mistake *once*."

Some time after the movie was finished, however, he made the same mistake once, and was married in New York. Monsignor David Spelgatti, the pastor of St. John the Evangelist Church on Main Street in Ishpeming, flew out to perform the ceremony. They had developed a close friendship.

There were numerous spur-of-the-moment parties among the cast, but Arthur and Jimmy seldom attended. They were much quieter than most of the rest. The cast was always nice enough to include me, though, which I loved. One party that Jimmy did attend, however, was a planned one at the Northland in Marquette. One of the costume staff, Vou Lee Giokaris, was leaving early as they no longer needed her, and they feted her with a get-together and dance in one of the private rooms.

I rode down with Boris Leven and his wife, who had accompanied him to the set location, and with Sam Leavitt, the cinematographer. They picked me up at home in one of the company vehicles.

We all joked and danced and, wonder of wonders, I danced with Jimmy twice, the only one he danced with! Such heaven!

I was walking on air when Sam accompanied me to my door after it was all over and we had driven the few miles back to Ishpeming.

The next day, "Where's your boyfriend?" Terri Hamilton teased, and many of the others joined in. It was such fun to be a star among stars!

Boris Leven's wife was amazed to learn, as we rode to the party in Marquette that evening, that I had never heard of a bagel. They were not available then in area stores, and while I had some Jewish friends they never mentioned bagels, although they may have eaten them at home.

"Meet me for breakfast in a few days. I'll order some from L.A. and we'll have a fine Jewish breakfast of bagels and lox.."

"I might as well admit it," I thought. So I bit the bullet, "I don't know what lox are either."

They all laughed at my culinary uneducated upbringing. Of course I knew what smoked salmon was, but had never heard it spoken of as lox.

A few days later she told me that the supplies had arrived, and we enjoyed a lovely breakfast of bagels, cream cheese and lox prepared for us by the chef.

At a later date she and Boris took Bill and me out to dinner at Oscar's Chalet, at the time considered the area's finest restaurant.. We had become good friends.

* * *

Gloria Stewart, Jimmy's wife, spent a couple of weeks at the hotel visiting her husband and friends in the cast. I met her under circumstances that weren't the best.

A large luncheon party was being held in the main dining room and we were serving the public in the Swiss Room. Charming though it was, this room, as I mentioned previously, was not adequate to be used as the main dining room in the evening while the movie people were there. Fortunately, though, this was lunch time, and since most of those involved were at the set, not many other guests showed up to star-watch.

At that time The Cleveland-Cliffs Iron Company executives often had lunch meetings at the hotel, and apparently one had been scheduled for that day, but I didn't know it. Something had slipped through the cracks and I hadn't been notified. Juel Casperson, the hotel manager, though a very nice man in many ways, could lose his temper quite easily. He lost it that day.

When the Cliffs group arrived there wasn't a table ready that was big enough to accommodate them. Storming about, shoving chairs and tables, Juel embarrassed everyone involved, and certainly me.

Suddenly I realized that the room was bustling with helpers. The Cliffs people scurried about, pushing tables together and moving chairs. Two of them were good friends of mine and fellow members, with my husband, of the Ishpeming Junior Chamber of Commerce, or Jaycees. (We still have a reunion each summer, but the number attending has now dwindled to just a few.) Sam Cohodas, owner of several local banks, was dragging chairs from other tables, and even Jim and Gloria Stewart pitched in.

After the situation had been remedied and everything was purring normally, Jim called to me in a voice no one in the small room could miss, least of all Mr. Casperson, who was still in the room visiting with the Cliffs people. "Joanie, come on over here and meet Gloria!"

Gloria was delightful. As down-to-earth and natural as an old shoe, she talked of her love of gardening and animals and how she enjoyed slopping around in jeans at home. She asked about my children and, as women who are mothers have a tendency to do, we exchanged notes about our kids. The Stewarts had twins.

Jimmy joined the crowd a lot while Gloria was there, laughing and joking and glancing at her with love in his eyes, but after she left he returned to his practice of only leaving his suite to dine. It was evident that they were a very happy, loving couple.

The company were all very generous about signing autographs, though they objected, rightfully so, to being disturbed during their meals. James Stewart objected at one other time also, and was criticized for it for years by the person involved.

Most Sundays he attended the Presbyterian Church just down the street from the back door of the Mather Inn. On one of these Sundays a woman, unfortunately a friend of mine, cornered him as he was entering the church. Jimmy ignored her and proceeded toward the church door, but she wouldn't take no for an answer. Finally, visibly annoyed by now, he signed his autograph without a word. Under better circumstances Jimmy would have exchanged a few pleasantries with the person for whom he was signing the autograph. The woman later told everyone that he had been rude to her, which really was quite the contrary. If there had been rudeness involved it was on the part of the intruder. After all, she was a grown woman at the time, several years older than I, and certainly should have known better than to pounce on a person who is going into a church. There are some things that should be kept private.

The movie that was the star's favorite was, surprisingly, a training film entitled "Winning Your Wings" made for the Air Force, then called the Army Air Corps. Jimmy was a pilot, and told me he had never been prouder of a film.

The maids all loved James Stewart, as he always treated them politely and in a friendly manner. One of them, an older woman, was extremely poor, supporting herself as best she could on her small hotel salary. Most salaries were very small in the nineteen fifties.

She did not own a radio, and would turn on Mr. Stewart's portable while she cleaned his suite. Once he happened to come back to his room while she was listening to it. The maid became very flustered and apologetic, but Jimmy told her she was perfectly welcome to play it whenever she wanted to.

When the movie was finished and Jimmy returned to Los Angeles, he left her the radio. How kind. As she told me about it, her eyes glistened with tears.

Murray Hamilton

I met Murray Hamilton and his wife Terri, a member of the former DeMarco Sisters singing group, by committing a faux pas.

Murray arrived somewhat later than most of the others as he wasn't scheduled for shooting right at the beginning. He and Terri came on an evening when the lobby was doing its usual high-jumps with people sitting, standing, visiting and laughing as they surreptitiously eyed the stars. While waiting for their bags, Murray and Terri took two seats near the front wall and just looked around, relaxing after the long train ride. Being a good hostess and trying to make everyone feel at home, I walked over to where they sat. I was sure they were local residents because he looked so familiar that I knew I had seen him often, probably on Main Street, maybe in the dime store.

"Hello," I greeted, and they replied in kind. "Did you come to see the movie people?"

They both chuckled, exchanging glances with smiling eyes, and Murray replied, "No. I'm in the picture."

Rightfully embarrassed, I started to apologize, mumbling something like, "But - oh, I'm sorry, I thought --."

"Don't worry about it," and he put me at ease with a wide smile. "It happens to me all the time. I've been in so many movies without having had big star billing that people think I'm an old acquaintance. It's one of those feelings of, 'I should know that guy, but from where?'"

We laughed, and my embarrassment disappeared.

As it turned out, Murray and I were in a scene together in the movie.

Kathryn Grant

Otto had said to me several times, "You are going to be in the picture." I thought it sounded like fun. Me in a movie!

He had a small part written in for me, that of a bar waitress, for a scene which was to take place in the bar where the actual murder had occurred. Hal Polaire, Mr. Preminger's assistant, asked, "Do you know how lucky you are? Why out in L.A. the starlets would be lined up for miles with necklines down to their waists to have Otto Preminger write in a part for them!"

I was to be paid $90.00 a day for three days, even though quite likely the filming would not take that long. This salary was a fortune in 1959, especially to people like us who were struggling to get through school and make ends meet. Another example of my experiences with Otto Preminger's generosity.

Early in the planning stages of the movie I overheard Henry Weinberger remark to Otto that in view of the poor economy of the area at the time, they could get by with paying the people less than they would have to pay in Hollywood. Mr. Preminger said strongly, "Ve vill pay them exactly what ve vould pay in California. No more -- and no less."

When the time came for "my" scene to be filmed, I got the star treatment and lapped it up like a kid does an ice cream cone.

Before the big day arrived I was fitted with a costume by Vou Lee Giokaris of the wardrobe staff. It was ostensibly a black skirt and white blouse, but the white blouse was really a light blue. In those days the black and white cameras did not photograph white very well and caused a glare, so anything that appeared white on screen was actually blue.

The day before each filming a call sheet was posted by the elevator in the lobby. It listed the date, the time of shooting, the set and scenes to be filmed, and any pertinent notes. The note for my day said, "All personnel leaving from the Mather Inn and Northland Hotel report promptly to the loading zone." Sounds like there were a few late-nicks.

Then there were lists of the artists, the characters they played, the time they were to report to makeup, their departure time, and the time they were to be on the set. Separate lists for directors and crew were at the bottom. I could hardly wait for it to be posted so I could see my name on a Carlyle Productions, Inc. call sheet. After much *casual* strolling past the elevator area , I found it. It read:

Artist	Character	In Makeup	Leave	On Set
JOAN LEHMANN	BAR GIRL	10:00	9:00	11:00.

Also on call that day were James Stewart, Kathryn Grant (Bing Crosby's wife), and Murray Hamilton.

When I reported the next morning I found that we would be late leaving as Kathryn Grant was in the makeup room at the hotel instead of having it done at the set as had been scheduled, and she and I were riding in the same car. While I waited she told me of her first meeting with Bing and how she had said to her grandmother, to whom she was very close, "I'm going to marry that man." True to her word.

. Miss Grant had a traveling companion, her sister-in-law Mrs. Grandstaff. Kathryn Grant's last name for movie purposes was a shortened version of Grandstaff, her maiden name. Her companion was married to Kathryn's brother.

The two started out by having their meals together, and would often split a cubed steak for breakfast. Later, though, Mrs. Grandstaff found a friend in Hal Polaire, the assistant director, and they often dined together. Kathryn, however, had many other friends she could join, so she was hardly lonely. Her sister-in-law left fairly soon, though, earlier than I thought had been planned. Perhaps Miss Grant decided that she wasn't really being a companion.

Kathryn Grant Crosby was striking in her looks. She had black hair which she tied back severely in a straight ponytail, the only break in the severity being a tiny curl at one side of her forehead. This she kept in place by painting it with a liquid which she ordered from France. She gave me some and I enjoyed experimenting with it.

CALL SHEET

CARLYLE PRODUCTIONS, INC.

PICTURE — "Anatomy of a Murder"   DATE WEDNESDAY, APRIL 29th 1959.

DIRECTOR — Otto Preminger   SHOOTING CALL 9:00 AM

SET & SCENES EXT. & INT. THUNDER BAY INN AND BAR. SC. 43,44,94.

NOTE: ALL PERSONNEL LEAVING FROM THE MATHER INN AND NORTHLAND HOTEL REPORT PROMPTLY TO THE LOADING ZONE.

ARTIST & (CHARACTER)		IN MAKEUP	LEAVE	ON SET
JAMES STEWART	PAUL	7:00	7:45	9:00
LEE REMICK	LAURA			NO CALL
ARTHUR O'CONNELL	PARNELL			NO CALL
EVE ARDEN	MAIDA			NO CALL
KATHRYN GRANT	MARY PILANT	10:00	9:00	11:00
MURRAY HAMILTON	PAQUETTE	8:45	7:45	9:00
RUSS BROWN	MR. LEMON			NO CALL
JOAN LEHMANN	BAR GIRL	10:00	9:00	11:00
	Desk Clerk			*Wardrobe*

ATMOSPHERE.

2	UTILITY STANDINS	8:00	
8	WOMEN	8:00	
8	MEN	8:00	
4	CHILDREN	8:00	

STANDINS.

PAUL'S CAR	TED NAPES	8:00
MAIDA'S CAR		

LEAVE

Cameraman (2)	7:00
Operator (3)	7:00
Asst. Cameramen	6:45
Electrician	6:30
Grips	6:30
Property Men	6:30
Set Dressers	6:30
Makeup	7:30 & 7:45
Hairdressers	7:30
Wardrobe Men	7:30
Wardrobe Women	7:30
Script Supervisor	
Teleprompter Opera.	
Mr. Preminger	7:00
Wally Weinberger	7:00
Max Slater	

LEAVE

Sound Mixer	7:00
Recorder	6:30
Boom Man	6:30
Cable Men	6:30
Special Effects	6:30
Painter	6:30
Craft Service	6:30
First Aid Man (2)	7:30
Unit Stillman	
Special Photog.	7:00
Art Director	
Dog Trainer	
Staff	6:30
Generator man	
Hope Bryce	8:00
Hal Pollaire	8:00

Her most compelling features were her eyes. They were huge and dark, and seemed to envelope her surroundings with a disturbing innocence.

One particular friend of Kathryn Grant was Orson Bean, the comedian and actor who played the part of the psychiatrist. Mr. Bean was later known as a regular contestant on Garry Moore's quiz show on television.

Miss Grant went to Mass on the mornings when her schedule would permit, and Orson Bean would accompany her, walking the few blocks to St. John's Catholic Church on South Main, the one whose pastor, Monsignor Spelgatti, performed Arthur O'Connell's marriage ceremony at a later date. In those days women were obliged to cover their heads on entering a Catholic church, and Miss Grant always wore a beautiful lace handkerchief.

She loved chocolates and was particularly fond of the freshly made varieties found at Donckers Candy and Gifts in Marquette. Her birthday present to Bing was a fishing net filled with a mixture from that confectioner. We all signed his card. On one occasion, Donckers sent her an enormous box of assorted candies and she left it open on a table in the dining room for everyone to share.

Just before the filming was to begin, Miss Grant had discovered that she was pregnant. She and Bing already had a son and were hoping for a daughter, especially since Bing had had only sons in his first marriage. Miss Grant referred to the child as Mary Frances. "Mary Frances is really growing," she would say. And, as many of us know, that same Mary Frances Crosby grew up to follow in her parents' footsteps by acting in movies.

* * *

And Mary Frances really was growing. Kathryn was, as she put it, ". . . definitely blossoming out." Vou Lee Giokaris had worked frantically to make two new dresses for Miss Grant for that scene, as it was the practice of the company to have two of each of the more important costumes available in case something disastrous happened to one of them. No one watching the movie would ever have suspected that this had been necessary, though. Miss Grant's figure was slim and beautiful.

We left, late, for Big Bay. Kathryn was very pleasant to chat with, and the hour or so ride was enjoyable. She was studying nursing at the time and was full of enthusiasm for her classes. I've always wondered, though, how she could manage it, since she was away so much.

"It looks like Godfrey has had it," she said, looking up from her newspaper. The announcement had just been made that the singer and talk show host, Arthur Godfrey, had been diagnosed with lung cancer. In 1959, lung cancer was almost always a death sentence. Happily, she was wrong. Godfrey lived a great many healthy and happy years after that diagnosis.

Upon arriving at the little town of Big Bay we were taken straight to the Big Bay Inn. Here I was directed to the room which had been turned into a beauty salon under the talented and experienced hands of Harry Ray, Del Armstrong and Myrl Stolz. I was treated to a make-over by Lana Turner's makeup man, Del Armstrong. Originally Lana Turner had been cast in the role of Laura Manion, wife of the alleged murderer, but she backed out. The reason given was that she didn't like the costumes, particularly the tight slacks. That may have been true. Who knows? It's hard, now, to imagine anyone but Lee Remick in that role, though. At any rate, Del Armstrong had already been hired, and he honored his contract.

Del was a very nice man, handsome and gentle. Those were lipstick-only days for most women in the U.P., and his artistry with cosmetics really made me look like a star. After he had finished, Myrl Stolz, the chief hairdresser, did my hair in a style completely new to me. I looked like someone else. Loved it.

When the call came to head for the set, I walked down the street with Jimmy Stewart.

"Meditate on your lines, Joanie," he teased. I didn't yet know what my lines even were, but I knew they wouldn't be much. Not that I cared. I was in the movies!

Three little girls stopped us and asked for our autographs.

"No-o-o, not me," I stammered. "I'm not an actress."

"Oh, come on, Joanie," Jimmy said in his wonderful drawl, "sign your name. You're the star of the picture." So I did, sheepishly.

When we got to the bar I was told by Mr. Preminger that the movie was getting much too long, over four hours at that point, and that my small part would have to be one of those being cut. I hadn't seen the part yet, but I imagine it would have been a few short words. "What'll you have?" Or something. But it was a bit disappointing not to be able to say those words, whatever they were.

"Lou is starting to tear his hair out," Mr. Preminger said wryly, referring to Louis Loeffler, the film editor who, with his son and his son's friend as learning apprentices, would have to cut the picture to a reasonable length without ruining its context. This was developing into a monumental task.

Mr. Preminger sat me in a booth facing the camera, with a male extra opposite me. We were warned not to look at the camera and to appear to be carrying on a conversation. Not easy to do without making a sound, but we managed. Jimmy came through the back door of the bar, the one that supposedly opened from the hotel, and strode past us to the bar itself behind which Murray Hamilton, who played the bartender, stood. After doing the entrance several times, Preminger, always the perfectionist, was satisfied and said, "Cut. Prrrint!" I did a little "business," though, which I thought was appropriate, and Otto didn't object. I'm sure he noticed, perfectionist that he was, but he must have thought it was okay. Each time Jimmy Stewart walked past our booth, on each subsequent take I turned slightly and glanced at him as he walked by. Most people do that when someone enters a room and walks past your table. Otto let me get by with it. My claim to stardom.

Paul Biegler, played by Jimmy, had come to the hotel to talk to its manager, Mary Pilant (Kathryn Grant), about the murder, since the murder victim had owned the hotel which Mary Pilant managed. After Paul spoke to the bartender for a few minutes, Mary entered. She and Paul sat down at a table.

Miss Grant did not know her lines. Hardly one.

If Preminger were ever going to blow his stack it would certainly have been at this time. But he kept his cool, don't ask me how. In later years I did a considerable amount of acting and directing myself, and I know I would have had to work hard to remain polite. He contained himself though, but his face was extremely taught, as was

Jimmy Stewart's.

After many failed attempts at rehearsal, Preminger had one of the assistant directors escort Miss Grant back to the hotel in order to drill her on her script. The rest of the cast and crew were left to wait. Production money was going out the window.

When Kathryn returned she was prepared, and the rehearsals and shooting went ahead.

First the scene was taken from behind Jimmy Stewart, focusing on Kathryn. This was done time after time until it won Otto's approval. Before each new take, Kathleen Fagan, the script supervisor, had to refill Jimmy's beer glass to the exact same level at which it had been at the beginning of the scene.

This angle completed, Sam Leavitt and his camera crew moved their equipment to a spot behind Kathryn, and the same procedure took place. There were several angles used, each requiring much time and precision.

Kathryn Grant was encouraged by Mr. Preminger with, "Don't forget, not only Gazzara has eyes!" And Miss Grant's eyes are spectacular in the entire movie, not just this scene.

In the picture Jimmy Stewart was required to smoke the brand of Italian cigar that John Voelker always smoked, as his role was actually that of the author. They were little ugly things, all gnarled and skinny, and smelled horrible. Jimmy could never manage to keep them lit, and this also added time to this scene as well as many others. (In those days they even smoked in the courtroom!) Finally the usually mild-mannered James Stewart blew up.

"These goddam cigars!" he blurted, staring at the end of the one he held in his hand with obvious distaste. Not like him, but it had been a trying day.

But a great day too. Duke Ellington arrived.

Duke Ellington

Edward Kennedy Ellington, the Duke, was in the process of writing the score for the picture and had come to Ishpeming to finish it in the proper atmosphere. He walked into the bar in Big Bay dressed in an elegant camel's hair coat, ankle-length and handsome, a silk scarf flowing from his shoulders. There was a hush in the room. Even Mr. Preminger seemed awed.

"Looks like we're making a movie here," Duke said, smiling almost shyly. One of Duke's most beautiful qualities, and there were many, was his voice. Soft yet compelling, it flowed over its listeners like a gentle waterfall, warming and soothing them.

"Ve hope so," replied Otto, shaking the Duke's hand.

Otto introduced everyone, even me, and Duke cordially acknowledged each introduction with a warm smile and a greeting. He said to me, "It's always a pleasure to meet a beautiful lady." I later read a quote from Lena Horne calling him a "snowman." Indeed he was. But snowman or not, I melted.

Mr. Preminger then showed him around the set, and after a short conversation Duke went back to his Carlyle Company car and was driven off. We all watched him go.

Duke Ellington had a presence which filled a room and took it over, and which left a void when he departed. His smile held a peaceful softness which made others feel relaxed and good. Duke was a star of the first kind. No one could doubt that.

I was through with my part of the filming at that point, and Bill had come to pick me up so I didn't have to wait for Miss Grant. Murray was also finished, and he rode back to Ishpeming with us.

It was an enjoyable ride. Murray told us tales of other movies he had been in, keeping us laughing all the way home. One of his favorites was The F.B.I. Story, in which he also acted with James Stewart. Murr was a great guy. Such a shame that he died so young.

Murray played the guitar and often entertained us at those impromptu get-togethers in the hotel. One night some of us were visiting and singing in the Elliott Room when Murray discovered that I had a pretty good singing voice. I had had some very good vocal training. I sang "Sometimes I Feel Like a Motherless Child" accompanied by Murray and his guitar, and it went very well. The company applauded exuberantly.

Otto seldom attended these impromptu get-togethers and Murray wanted him to hear me sing, so the next time we had a sing-along he went and got Otto.

"Wait 'til you hear this girl sing," he told the director as he picked up his guitar.

I froze. I was going to sing for Otto Preminger! At that moment I was sure I couldn't even talk, much less sing. The time we had done it before it had been completely impromptu and the song had just flowed naturally. Now it had become a performance. My heart pounded.

We did the same number, but believe me it wasn't at all the same. I clutched up in the presence of the great man. I sang okay. That was it. Just okay. Later Murray said to me, "You didn't sing it like you did last time." He didn't have to tell me. I knew. In later years I did a lot of singing and acting, but I never had a worse case of stage fright than I did that night.

* * *

The next time I saw Duke he was sitting at the baby grand piano in the hotel's main dining room. The waitresses and I were taking care of the final preparations before opening the Georgian Room doors, and Duke asked us what we would like to hear. One of the girls, obviously not an Ellington connoisseur, asked if he would play "Sweet Georgia Brown", the theme song of the Harlem Globetrotters basketball team.

The Duke didn't raise an eyebrow, but I did see a small twinkle in his eyes as he replied, "Well, I can try." "Sweet Georgia Brown" was not really Duke's style. Always a gentleman though, he played the song.

Then he looked at me and asked, "What would you like to hear?" I asked for one of my favorites of his compositions, "Mood Indigo," and he looked more at home. I had first heard this song when I was about eight or nine years old, and had loved it ever since. What a thrill to hear it played by the composer -- and for me!

Duke composed at the baby grand piano in the dining room, usually late at night. Not much of a drinker, he would sometimes order a gin and tonic, but only one. Often we would chat for a while as I finished up my work and later, after we got to know each other better, we would occasionally play the piano together.

There in the dining room, at that piano, was captured the essence of Ishpeming, which became the essence of the score of "Anatomy of a Murder."

* * *

Another industry besides mining which existed in Ishpeming in 1959 was the Gossard factory which made ladies' undergarments. This had been the principal source of jobs for women of the area for many years.

The building which housed the factory was, and is, one of the largest in town, occupying most of a block and boasting three stories. Later a basement cafeteria would be added. At three o'clock when the day's work ended, the workers would stream out of "The Gossard" and down the streets, filling the grocery stores and downtown shops.

The Gossard was known as an unending source of town gossip, as the women exchanged the latest while they sewed at their machines. The hospital, just a couple of blocks away, was not far behind. One woman was heard to say, "I know it's true. It's hospital gossip straight from Gossard gossip."

The Gossard had a handsome clock atop its third floor which chimed the hours. It was a comforting sound, one we all knew and loved. Duke must have loved it as we did, because he included it in one of the numbers of the score, giving it the haunting title of "Midnight Indigo." In its notes can be heard the tones of the Gossard clock and can be felt the crispness of the cold night air as between them they wrapped themselves around the silence of an Ishpeming night in spring.

Anyone who knows Grace Voelker would easily find her in Duke's "Grace Valse." Her quiet gentleness flows with the notes. Duke was very fond of Grace.

I'm in one of the numbers, too, entitled "Flirtibird."

Duke was amused by my walk. It's kind of an odd one, I guess. Not the epitome of grace, that I know. I had to do a lot of puttering around while preparing the dining room for each meal, and Duke was often at the piano as I worked.

One day he said, "You're going to be in my music, you know."

I stopped, turned to him, and said incredulously, "I am?" A trained musician myself and later to take my studies much further, Duke had always been one of my idols.

"You are." And he began to play. "It's your walk," he told me. "It will be played on the saxophone."

He would often play it as I moved around the dining room checking everything out to be sure it was ready for the next opening. We would both laugh at my inability not to walk to its notes. I still get nostalgic when I hear it, and I miss Duke.

* * *

On Mother's Day Bill sent me a corsage, quite a beautiful surprise, especially in view of our tight circumstances. Duke asked, "Are you a mother?"

I told him I was.

"You're not only beautiful, you're glorious," he told me, giving me a hug.

Duke was sincerely religious, though I never knew him to attend a church. He was also very family-oriented. He wore a gold cross and chain around his neck that his sister had given him for his birthday when they were both children. In later years he composed some breathtaking instrumental and choral pieces which were based on God and religion.

Loving his generous tips, the waitresses took turns delivering Duke's dinners to his room. He was on a diet, and always ordered two halves of grapefruit and two baked potatoes to accompany the huge New York strip steaks he had shipped in almost daily. The steaks looked like roasts. A diet??

In the movie, Jimmy Stewart plays one of Duke's compositions entitled "Happy Anatomy." Jimmy had already begun to learn the song before he arrived in Ishpeming but asked me to help him with it, and we would play it as a duet. I also played it with Duke. It's a light-hearted, fun tune which Jimmy plays in one of the Voelker home scenes and as a duet with Duke at Mount Shasta ..

The credits of the movie open with Ray Nance's trumpet playing a wailing call as though summoning someone. Duke said he was calling, "Joanie." He may have just been kidding me, but whenever I hear it, I hear my name.

The band rehearsed in the dining room when it was closed between meals, and what a treat it was. A Duke Ellington concert every day! I felt very lucky.

One morning some of Duke's staff who were staying at the Northland came to the Inn for breakfast. With them was Billy Strayhorn, Duke's arranger and fellow composer. Many of the songs attributed to the Duke were actually composed by Billy, such as "Take the 'A' Train" and "Lush Life," or were collaborations with Billy, as was "Satin Doll."

I gave them menus and asked if I could get them coffee. Billy, a very nice looking, soft-spoken small man wearing horn-rimmed glasses, told me, "No, but you can bring me a martini." He looked more like a college professor than a guy who'd be ordering a martini for breakfast.

This was a first for me. I was twenty-six years old, it must be remembered, and hardly drank except occasionally when the boss was off playing bridge and a waitress would bring me, with a wink, a Manhattan in a coffee cup. (Can't stand the things now. Billy had the right idea!) I guess I must have looked at him with a touch of surprise, because he laughed.

When Billy left to take the train back to Chicago a few weeks later, I had the kitchen prepare a lunch for him as the night train did not have a restaurant car, and I put in a couple of cigarettes. Smoking had not as yet become tabu, and the dining room offered cigarettes to its guests. Billy expressed his appreciation over and over as her prepared to leave for the depot.

One time one of the band members reported for rehearsal a bit drunk. I could see by the look on Duke's face that he was not happy about this.

He said to the band, as he often did, "Well, are you ready to play?" But he usually said it with his happy smile. This time there was no smile. They had an especially long and grueling session that day. With Duke you didn't mix work and play.

On the night that Duke was to leave, he said goodbye to all of us in the lobby and exited the hotel with his graceful, confident stride to walk the half block to the depot. I felt a lump in my throat. I would miss my good friend.

I heard the train whistle in from the roundhouse. A few minutes later it whistled out of Ishpeming.

And then, suddenly, there was Duke coming through the door. He hurried to me, saying, "I just had to have one more goodbye," and kissed me on the cheek. "Have to hurry. The train won't wait too long." In a breeze he was gone once again.

I learned later that he had talked the conductor into having the train backed up for him. Duke could charm anyone. Lena Horne's snow-man. But what a beautiful blizzard.

Before his stay in Ishpeming was completed, Duke had invited Bill and me to be his guests at the Blue Note in Chicago, so we saved every penny we could spare in order to be able to afford the trip We took the "sleeper" train down, having reserved one of the small bedrooms, the kind that had a toilet under one of the bunks. Needless to say, this was not the most convenient arrangement when the bunk was made up for the night, but better than nothing. After we had boarded, the porter told us that no one had booked the roomette, and asked us if we would like it for $1.00 more. We didn't have much money, but couldn't resist.

I was so excited at the prospect of seeing Duke again and hearing his music that I hardly slept that night, and spent it watching towns and fields and trees fly by and listening to the signals clang past, peeling out their bing-bing-baaaaang-bing.

We stayed at Duke's favorite Chicago hotel, the Sherman. Over-looking beautiful Lake Michigan, it was one of the grande dames of the Chicago hotels.

After checking in and having a bite to eat, Bill and I went to a base-ball game. When it was over we took a walk to do a little window shopping and to gaze up, like the small-town kids we were, at the tall buildings. Chicago *is* a wonderful town! Suddenly we heard, "Joanie! Hi, Joanie!" Down the street, waving frantically, was Billy Black, Duke's promotion man. He had stayed at the Northland during the filming, as had Duke's band members, but they came to the Inn to rehearse and often to eat, so I knew them all quite well.

Billy Black asked, "Does the Duke know you're here?"

"We left a note in his box at the hotel," I told him.

"I'll make sure he knows," Billy promised. "You're to be his guests, you know."

It was disconcerting, though, during our conversation on that busy Chicago street in the summer of 1959, to see the glances thrown our way by a few of the passersby, as we, two white people, chatted with Billy, a black man. Some of the darting looks held disgust, some almost fury. Bill and I were not used to that kind of hate, having been raised in little Ishpeming.

When we returned to the hotel we found a note from Duke in our mailbox. It read, "Bill & Joan Lehman[n], 1538, Will make your reservations for tonight -- you are my guests -- see you there, Greetings, Duke E."

After a nice dinner at the hotel we took a taxi to the famous Blue Note, showplace of the greats of the jazz and blues world. I had seen Sarah Vaughn there when I visited my cousin in Chicago at the age of seventeen.

The Blue Note, on the second floor of the building, did not take reservations. It was first-come-first-serve, and there was a line-up all the way down the narrow stairway and out onto the sidewalk. Feeling a little embarrassed, Bill and I slithered past the waiting crowd to a few catcalls and snide remarks, finally reaching the doorman at the top of the stairs. Bill told him, "I'm Bill Lehmann. We have reservations."

"We don't take reservations," was the rather aloof reply.

"Duke said he would make one for us."

This brought a huge change in the man's attitude. "Oh, *you're* the people! Welcome to the Blue Note. Come right this way."

Past table after table he led us, right to the front of the large room and right to Duke Ellington's ringside. We felt like celebrities.

Duke waved at us, and as soon as the number they were playing had finished, he began "Happy Anatomy," calling out to me, "You should be playing this!"

Billy Strayhorn sat with us for a while, again thanking me for the lunch, and other band members stopped by. The show was, of course, superb, an experience never to be forgotten.

The following Christmas, and every Christmas thereafter until he died, we received a gigantic and elaborate card from the Duke addressed in his own big, sprawling hand.

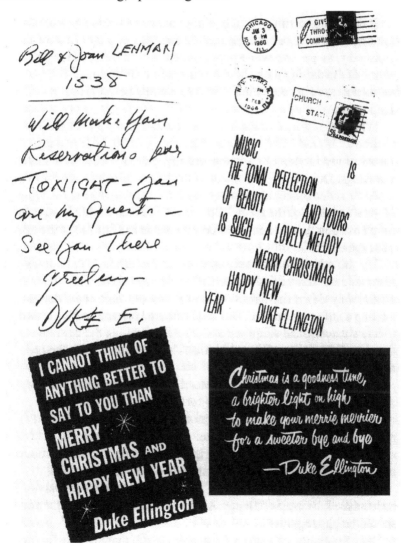

Eve Arden, Brooks West and the Welches

Eve Arden was always knitting -- in the dining room, while waiting on the set, in the lobby. Most of her knitting was for her children, and believe me they had some spectacular sweaters, lucky kids.

She had been unable to become pregnant for a long time, but then, she told me, "We crossed to Europe on an ocean liner to make a picture and all the juices must have started flowing." She came home expecting a child. They had several.

Those who have loved Eve Arden on the screen over the years would have had no trouble loving her in person. Down to earth, matter of fact, and unassumingly friendly, she captured all of our hearts. The clipped manner of speaking which we heard in her movies was the same manner she used with all of us, always with a chuckle behind her words which gave the impression that she was hiding a laugh.

Her husband, Brooks West (hence the later television show "Our Miss Brooks," which starred Miss Arden), played the part of the district attorney. John based this character on the man who in real life had previously defeated him for the office of prosecutor. This character does not come across as a very competent lawyer either in the book or in the movie. John got even.

Brooks used to give me an envelope with money in it every week. In fact, I did quite well over and above my $150.00 a month (before deductions) salary. I received gifts from Carlyle Productions each week as well as from Mr. Welch, who played the judge.

The Wests were both lovely people, the kind you enjoy knowing.

* * *

Mr. and Mrs. Welch had been married just three weeks when they came to Ishpeming. They were both widowed and had been close friends as a foursome when their spouses were alive, so decided to get married. It was fun to watch them look fondly into each other's eyes. Such a happy couple.

Mr. Welch was well known as the counsel for the Army in the McCarthy hearings which had been in the news for such a long time previously. Clips of it are still occasionally shown in documentaries.

"I've always wanted to be a judge," he told me. "So now I at least get to pretend I'm one." Nonetheless, we all called him "Judge."

Agnes Welch played one of the jurors. Sitting prominently on the end in the front row and wearing a perky little hat, she gave the perfect impression of a dainty small-town lady.

Hats were important parts of a woman's wardrobe in the fifties. You weren't completely dressed up without one. The audience in the courtroom scenes is a sea of hats. It is also a sea of men wearing suits and ties, something that has now become more the exception than the rule.

George C. Scott

George C. Scott was new to movies when he played the lawyer from Lansing, the capital of Michigan, who was brought in by the prosecution to assist at the trial. Though he has since done numerous films, he didn't like them then. He would say, "The stage is the only place for real acting, and summer stock is the only training."

During the filming he and Preminger often had disagreements, though both did their best to hold their tempers. Back at the hotel, however, George would drown his sorrows quite heavily in the bar. He also gambled heavily, as did many of the men in the company. Sometimes one of them would lose his whole week's pay and have to ask for credit in the bar and dining room, a practice frowned upon by Carlyle Productions. George had children to support from previous marriages, and this posed a very real problem at times.

He worried about his drinking and talked to me about it once. However he never drank during working hours and was always well prepared and alert to every nuance while on the set. If his drinking was a problem, it was a problem only to himself. He never inflicted its consequences on others.

Bill and I occasionally had a drink with him in the Tap Room on my day off. He was very much fun to be with.

The first time we sat with him I asked, "What else have you been in?" He was pretty much a newcomer then.

"Most recently a Playhouse 90 with Teresa Wright," he said. "Shortly before I came here."

Those were the days of live television, and Playhouse 90 was, in Bill's and my opinion, one of the best. Sets wiggled on occasion, or even fell over, actors muffed their lines and were bailed out by fellow players, and other near-disasters occurred, but it was real. I could see why George liked it. It was the stage. A stage which those of us who did not live in New York or other large cities could enjoy and love.

Of course, being so busy and working so late because of the movie, I no longer had much opportunity to watch television. But before the filming started I would get home fairly early. The Mather Inn was then primarily a salesman and businessman hotel (and yes, in those prehistoric days they were "sales*men* and business*men*!), and those working guests ate early dinners and retired soon after to get ready for the next day's work. A few frequented the bar later, but that didn't affect me. I could leave as soon as the dining room closed, even if there were still some guests lingering over coffee or after-dinner drinks. Thus I had seen the Playhouse 90 in question, remembered Teresa Wright (who could forget that smile?), but was sure I hadn't seen George.

"What role did you play?" I asked, a bit embarrassed at not knowing.

"The sheriff," he told me.

I couldn't believe it. Remembering the mean, nasty sheriff who had turned out to be the culprit, I stared at George. Yes. The two were one and the same. George's excellent acting in the television role had completely transformed him into another person, one nothing like his real self. It was amazing.

Bill must have felt as I did. He said, "Well I'll be darned. I didn't even recognize you."

George smiled, pleased. "I guess that means I did a pretty good job of acting, maybe? Fooled you guys, anyway."

"You sure did," I agreed, impressed. "I didn't recognize you either. Great job, Georgie. We loved the show." (I'll explain the "Georgie" later.)

"Playhouse 90 is one of the best," he said, mimicking our own thoughts.

* * *

At the time, George was dating Colleen Dewhurst, the two having not yet entered into their fiery marriage. This was still the days of hotel lobby switchboards, and of course switchboard operators were wont to listen in on occasion. With so many movie people as guests, what a temptation!

George received many calls from Colleen, and placed many to her. During one of them the switchboard operator "mistakenly" (!!) opened the key and heard George say, "I was in the shower."

The reply was, "Oh, is that great big beautiful body all naked and dripping?" Nothing remarkable by today's standards, but juicy gossip in the fifties.

George asked me if I had heard of Miss Dewhurst. I hadn't. At that time she was acting mostly on the stage. He told me, "She's the best of any of the new actresses. Has them all beat." I later came to agree.

"Is she coming to visit you?" I asked. Many spouses and friends came for short stays.

"In a couple of weeks. I want you to meet her."

"I'll look forward to it."

I first met her at breakfast when I seated her at a table for two near a window that looked out toward the porch.

"Thank you," she said politely, turning to look up at me. And there was that glorious smile gleaming as brightly as the sun that was flashing through the window panes. Not beautiful by movie star standards, she was more beautiful than any of the other stars when she smiled. That same smile has captivated many audiences over the years.

As with Hope Bryce, Colleen could not openly stay in George's room, so an elaborate story was circulated that she would room with one of the women. The hotel was full, so she couldn't be given a separate room. Of course this fooled no one, but it satisfied the proprieties.

It was obvious to all of us that George was very much in love with Colleen. He did much less drinking while she was here.

They later married and, unfortunately, were eventually divorced.

Ben Gazzara

Ben Gazzara was a flirt. What girl, married or single, young or old, doesn't like to be flirted with? Not me, anyway.

"Are you married, Joanie?" he asked shortly after he arrived.

"Yes I am."

Leaning on his elbows on my cashier's desk, his face level with mine, he stared at me with those penetrating eyes. I drowned in them. He asked, "How married *are* you, Joanie?"

My breath caught.

But of course I *was* married, and so replied banteringly, "Pretty married, Bennie."

That started something. Someone of the company must have overheard it because soon George C. Scott was "Georgie" and Duke Ellington became "Dukie." Even Mr. Preminger picked it up. "Hello, Georgie," he would say, or, to John, "How are you today, Judgie?" John Voelker loved calling Ellington "Dukie," and much later wrote a piece about the composer entitled "Dukie." No one seemed to know how those nicknames got started, but I did. It began with, "How married *are* you, Joanie?" "Pretty married, Bennie."

No one called Mr. Preminger "Ottoie," though. He was much too formidable for that.

One of my most hated tasks at the hotel was to have to fire someone. Hiring was fun. Firing was not.

I had hired one young girl who just wasn't working out. She was often late, one time just didn't show up, and was not proving to be a good waitress. Juel ordered, "You'll have to dismiss her." Again I got the fun jobs.

I plowed through it as best I could, trying not to hurt her feelings too badly, and advertised for a replacement. Understandably, given the economy of our area and the fact that the hotel was swarming with famous people, we were swamped with applications. Among others, an old friend called for an appointment.

"I really could use a job, Joanie," she told me at our interview.

I knew that she had had waitressing experience, and I also knew that she would present well to the guests. She was a beautiful young woman, a year or two older than I, with shiny black hair and a smile that lit her whole face. I hired her.

She worked out very well. For about two weeks.

Then she came to me. "I have back trouble, Joanie. Have had it for years. I just can't carry those heavy trays anymore."

Of course one wonders why, if she had back trouble, she applied for a job as a waitress. But anyway. Not for me to question.

"I'm sorry to see you leave," I said, meaning it. Now I would have to go through another bunch of interviews. And she had definitely been an asset to the dining room.

But I knew what the real story was. She had met Bennie. Mission accomplished.

Lee Remick

Lee Remick arrived wearing a long fur coat and carrying her very young baby. Her beauty caught every eye in the lobby as she spoke to the desk clerk, tossing her shiny reddish-blond hair in a gesture which was to become familiar to all who would know her. She was to occupy two rooms, one for herself and the other serving as quarters for the baby's nurse.

This was to be her first starring role and she acted the part, making grand entrances wherever she went. She was thoroughly enjoying the heady experience of being a star, though not really offensive about it. I'm sure she toned down as stardom became less of a novelty. Lee Remick certainly did some fine acting over the years.

Shortly after her arrival she stopped me in the lobby and asked, "Do you know of anyone who could loan me a baby carriage for the time I'm here?"

I did, of course, and said I would arrange it. Some friends obliged, and the nurse was able to take the baby for its daily fresh air walk.

Miss Remick was very careful about what she ate and drank, only occasionally joining the rest in a drink, a rye old fashioned. As she sometimes remarked, "I have to get into those tight slacks, you know." She definitely looked great in them though, so her abstemiousness paid off.

Gjon Mili, an award-winning "Life Magazine" photographer, was doing the black and white still promotional photos for the movie. He would snap the cast in the bar before dinner, in the lobby, and in the dining room. He also, of course, did posed stills that pertained to the plot.

Mr. Mili was a cantankerous Viennese. He answered most questions and replied to most conversational endeavors with barely a nod, and sometimes a growl. He was not a friendly person, to say the least.

I probably came the closest of any to seeing him soften. He walked into the closed and deserted dining room one evening as I was playing "Vienna, My City of Dreams" on the baby grand.

Looking lonely he said, "That brings back my childhood. Reminds me of home."

Sitting down at one of the tables, he stayed until I had finished the piece.

That mood did not last, however.

One night shortly after, he entered the dining room with his camera and began taking random shots of those who were still lingering there, including Miss Remick.

Then he stopped at the area where she was sitting and began taking picture after picture of her only.

Those at her table watched, smiling, as she acted for the camera. She ran her fingers through her beautiful hair and threw it back with a snap of her head, leaning backward as though feeling a cool breeze touch her face. She smiled. She didn't smile. She crossed her legs. She uncrossed her legs. Each new pose seemed to become more innocently sensual. Her enjoyment of the attention was obvious. Why not? She was the star.

And then Mili stopped, looked gravely at his camera and said in his Viennese accent, "Oh damn, dere's no film in da camera." With an exaggerated look of pain in his eyes, he left.

Miss Remick, laughing in obvious embarrassment as we all squirmed in sympathy, visited briefly with her table-mates and left the dining room. True she was enjoying her new-found status, but she was not harming anyone with her exuberance. Such an insult should have been left undone.

I watched Lee Remick on the set several times, and it was obvious that this young woman was a fine actress. Her future successes were not surprising.

Lee's father came to visit for a while. I first met him at a party at the Roosevelt Bar, a pub and dance hall owned by Anthony "Gigs"

Gagliardi, a very close friend and fishing buddy of John Voelker. Lee and her father entered the back room where we were gathering, most of us not yet seated, and she began introducing him. When she came to me, she waved a hand in the air and said breezily, "Oh, everybody knows Joanie." Of course it was obvious that her dad, since this was his first visit to Ishpeming, did not know me. A real brush-off.

John, seated at the center of a long table by the wall, heard and called out, "Joanie, come on over here and sit by Uncle John. Sit at my right," and he pulled out the chair next to him. After the brush-off, I became the guest of honor! "Uncle John" wasn't about to suffer any cuts to one of his West Barnum Street Irishers.

As always I didn't stay long at the party, and excused myself to go to the bar in the front of the building and call a cab. My home was a much longer walk from the Roosevelt than it was from the Mather Inn. Del Armstrong, the makeup man who had transformed me in Big Bay, noticed and offered to get one of the company cars and drive me home. I accepted. I can see why Lana Turner wanted him exclusively as her makeup man. A very nice person. And he really wasn't flirting. Just being nice.

Lee Remick's father was rumored to have been very wealthy. If this was true, he certainly didn't throw his money around. He would stay down in the bar drinking with the rest, and every once in a while would come up to the dining room and fill a plate from the snack table, taking that food back to the Tap Room with him and never buying a dinner.

Mr. Casperson stood it for as many evenings as he could. Finally he came to me and said, "We're going to have to charge him for the hors d'oeuvres." I knew what was coming. "Go down and tell him." Yet another fun thing I got lucky enough to do.

I weaseled around it though. I had one of the waitresses prepare a bill and just take it down and hand it to him. Sneaky!

But it worked. After that he had dinner in the Georgian Room like everybody else. And paid for it.

Before Lee Remick left she sent a very nice thank-you note to my friends from whom I had borrowed the carriage.

David and Patricia Silver

David Silver was the first assistant director. His wife, Pat, stayed with him throughout the filming. Dave was Jewish and Pat was Irish.

Pat had been born in Ireland, and I enjoyed hearing her tales of the country of my ancestors.

On one of my Fridays off I invited her to my home for lunch. She told me of how she had had to begin studying to be a nun because there was no money for college any other way. This was not for her, though. She came to the United States as some of her brothers had done, hoping to find work. The farm in Ireland had been divided about as many times as it could handle, and the younger boys had to leave. It could not support them all.

Pat was unbelievably beautiful, in fact stunning. She had the light Irish complexion and golden red hair which together make heads turn. Not surprisingly, the work she found was in modeling.

"But I hate standing in those unemployment lines," she told me that day.

My eyebrows hastened upwards. "You stand in unemployment lines?" I asked. Her husband was Otto Preminger's number one assistant director, and they had to be far from poor.

"Of course," she said. "I can't always find work, and I'm eligible for it. Why not?"

I guess she had a point. She had, of course, earned it.

We had a vodka martini and a simple lunch of a casserole and some rolls I had made. It was a very pleasant visit.

Dave invited me to come over and watch the filming of the railroad scene at the depot near the hotel, and I walked over between my meal shifts. The large crew was bustling about as usual, moving cameras, checking sound equipment and discussing various aspects of the scene in order to decide which would be the best way to achieve the desired results.

In spite of all the talent and expertise with which he was surrounded, Mr. Preminger always had the final say. It was his picture. Everyone knew that, and deferred to his wishes. Perhaps that accounted for the lack of tension and confrontation during the making of the movie.

They were filming the arrival of Orson Bean, playing the army psychiatrist Dr. Smith, who had examined Lieutenant Manion (Ben Gazzara) to determine whether he was of sound mind at the time of the murder. The defense would, as was to be expected, plead insanity.

Carlyle Productions had arranged to have a train and its crew for the scene. The big engine sailed in with its passenger cars in tow, the horn blowing a song of arrival. After it slowly ground to a stop, Orson Bean emerged. Then Orson Bean would turn around and climb the steps into the car once more, the train would back out, and the scenario would be repeated. And repeated. It must have been performed at least ten times, quite likely more than that. Mr. Preminger just wasn't satisfied.

Sam Leavitt, the cinematographer, wasn't either. He too sought perfection. The sun wasn't exactly right. He didn't like the angle. Another take was necessary.

Among the many experts chosen by Mr. Preminger to guide his movie was the sound engineer, Jack Solomon. This was a difficult scene for him with all the background noise as the train chugged into the station, its wheels rolling and clanging, finally coming to a loud and screaming halt. He was not satisfied. Again another take.

The scene had to become a "print" before the light was lost. Spring's hours of sunshine up here are short, and they didn't want that scene to go over into the following day. The production schedule was very tight. Another day of shooting would not only throw off the schedule but would cause added expense.

They did finish it, though. I couldn't stay for the cut-print as I had to return to the dining room, but when they returned Sam Leavitt said in his usual unsmiling way, "Well, Joanie, we did it. It's a wrap." He was obviously relieved.

Sam Leavitt had been nominated for an Oscar that year for "The Defiant Ones." We all awaited the award ceremony eagerly, wishing Sam well, patting his back in encouragement, and calling him our star. Since our U.P. television was not as sophisticated then as it has since become, we had to wait for news broadcasts either on television or radio. Finally the word came. Someone burst into the dining room crying, "He won! He won!"

Sam was our hero then. Everyone flocked to him, hugging him, shaking his hand, shouting congratulations. We were all delighted. So, to say the least, was Sam. His usually rather stern visage beamed at the adulation.

The Ishpeming and Marquette newscasts played it up big. Our newspaper, "The Daily Mining Journal," went into ecstasies. We had a genuine Academy Award winner in our midst! Ishpeming was on the map for something besides our beloved ski jumping.

With us at that time also were several other luminaries. Included among many Oscar winners and nominees in the past were Otto's nomination for"Laura," James Stewart's Oscar for "The Philadelphia Story" and nominations for "It's a Wonderful Life" and "Harvey," Arthur O'Connell's nomination for "Picnic," and Boris Leven's long list of nominations for art direction including an Academy Award for "West Side Story." More would come for most of them in later years.

The Orson Bean scene was not the only one filmed at the Ishpeming depot, a place which was very familiar to me as a child since I had taken the train to visit my father on many occasions. The scene depicts Arthur O'Connell and James Stewart waiting to pick up Ben Gazzara as he returns from being examined by the psychiatrist.

The building was typical of most small town depots in those days, with its chalkboard schedule hanging near the door and its candy and peanut machines which dispensed, not bags of munchies as they do today, but rather handfuls. (Deliver us from the Food and Drug Administration!) Old railroad pictures lined the walls and long benches reminiscent of church pews marched across the center of the room. The old warped wooden floor creaked and groaned, wiggling menacingly with each step taken over it.

Ishpeming Train Station
by Connie Langson, 1991,
National Mine School

Our cozy old depot is gone now, having given way to a new street, and the passenger trains have given way to airplanes. With the freight train tracks now outside the city we no longer hear that wonderful soulful cry of the horn as they creep through our town, a cheerful call by day and a haunting one at night. With the passing of the years we have gained so much, and also lost so much.

Mount Shasta

I wasn't able to watch the filming at Mount Shasta Restaurant, though Sam had invited me to do so.

"Shasta" is a very attractive log building with a fairly large dining room, a bar area, an alcove for more private dining, and a kitchen so clean that the door is never shut. At the time of Anatomy there wasn't even a door to close. Its owners over the years have always kept it very attractively decorated inside, and brightened outside by colorful flower box arrangements during the summer months and appropriate seasonal and holiday decorations in the winter. It beckons passersby with a cozy welcome.

In 1992 Walter and I decided to sell our home in Ishpeming and make our "camp" on Lake Michigamme (pronounced Mish-u-gahm'-ee), our year-round home. In our area any second or summer home is called a camp, though some are mansions. Ours was a camp, but definitely not a mansion! It was located at the far east end of the lake near Van Riper Park and Campground, while Shasta is across the highway at the west end, just outside the town of Michigamme itself.

We spent a great deal of time at Shasta, in summer getting there by boat and docking at one of the two courtesy docks provided by the owners, and in winter by the often treacherous method of guiding the car over icy roads. But the time for Walter to retire arrived, and gradually the years caught up with us. The long drives, snow shoveling, and all the other inescapable chores which accompany a home became more and more tiring as we added those years to our lives. Though it was a difficult decision to make, we finally moved to an apartment in nearby Marquette. Two years after Walter's death I moved to assisted living, where I now reside. A lot of years have floated away since I first applied to Juel Casperson for that Mather Inn job!

The winters are as beautiful out there as are the summers. Snowmobiles go by on the lake, we had squirrels and nuthatches at our feeders and deer in our yard, and one year moose from Canada were dropped in our area, and buses were supplied at Van Riper Park to transport the "moose watchers" to the site and thus avoid the congestion which would accompany so many cars.

In the Mount Shasta scene, Duke Ellington and James Stewart play "Happy Anatomy" together on the old upright piano. This is the song I played with both of them in the Georgian Room. In that scene Shasta is filled with people dancing, most of them natives of Michigamme or the nearby and equally small town of Champion, which is down at our end of the lake. One of the dancers, Stella Ball, later became the owner of the restaurant along with her husband, Bob. At the time of the making of Anatomy, Shasta was owned by Bob's parents, Maurice and Norma Ball.

As the scene opens, Lee Remick is drinking and dancing while her husband sits in jail. This is much to the disapproval of their lawyer, Jimmy Stewart, who is at the piano with Duke Ellington. The Duke's movie name is Pie-Eye, which can be seen on one of the drums, a nickname he used for some people. I was "Joanie-Pie."

James seeks Lee out and escorts her firmly from the dance floor and out the door. The next scene takes place in his convertible in the parking lot of Mt. Shasta. Both inside and out, the building looks much the same now as it did then.

The Crash

When Arthur O'Connell's crash scene was to be filmed at Big Bay, the Mather Inn catered dinner for the company in the school gymnasium. During normal shooting days we only catered lunch (those go-dawful ones in Tom's song!), but since it was necessary to shoot this scene during darkness, dinner was loaded into our catering truck and transported to Big Bay.

I accompanied the caterers to the set on my day off, ostensibly in order to help out but in truth I wanted to watch the filming. Once again my darling aunts were willing to baby-sit, since Bill had just begun working evenings for Cliffs along with continuing his education at Northern Michigan University.

Truck after truck arrived and workers began setting up equipment. The fence was erected into which O'Connell would crash, and all the other props were set up for the shooting.

James Stewart's stand-in was to do the actual driving when the car really did crash, with shots of Arthur O'Connell substituted later.

Finally the grips had everything ready. The elaborate set was in place. Sam Leavitt climbed onto his moveable camera dolly and Otto Preminger took his place on another. Dave Silver cried, "Roll 'em!" The take was numbered. One. The car began to move, slowly at first, then faster and faster. Through the fence it flew and into a barn door. Then it stopped. I can't figure out to this day how they did it without squashing Jimmy Stewart's stand-in. But out he climbed and walked away.

Otto conferred with his directors of photography and sound and with assistant director Dave Silver. They nodded, they pointed, they scratched heads and chins. During this conference the grips were setting up the scene again. None of them was optimistic enough to believe that the first take would be the final one. They were right.

Back into the car climbed Jimmy's stand-in. The motor churned. Take two.

Again I didn't count the number of takes that was required to get a "print," but it was many. Finally, though, as with all the scenes, it was finished. In the movie it's really quite spectacular, especially to someone who has watched the filming as I had.

Then we all returned to the school where the hotel staff had filled long buffet tables with a variety of foods and beverages. The cast and crew were tired. They ate quickly and got into their cars for the trips back to the Mather Inn in Ishpeming and the Northland Hotel in Marquette.

Lawrence Paquin

A name which is not too familiar to most movie-goers but which would be very well known in theater circles is that of Lawrence Paquin. Mr. Paquin acted and directed on Broadway, toured with many well-known actors and actresses, and was the first director of the "Voice of America" radio program. He also taught at Duke University and was, for a time, principal of the high school in the town in which he was born, Michigamme.

Mr. Paquin plays one of the jurors in Anatomy, and in the final courtroom scene we see him as the jury foreman who gives the verdict of not guilty.

I first met Mr. Paquin in the early 1970's when I was still active in our local theater group, Marquette Community Theater. Rowland Gustafson, who was president of our group at the time, called Bill and me and asked if we would take a Michigamme gentleman to dinner at the Northwoods Supper Club and then to a play, Man of LaMancha, which M.C.T. was staging in one of the large private rooms of that restaurant. It was summer at the time, and since Bill, (my first husband) and I were living at our camp on Lake Michigamme, Gus thought it logical that we should escort Mr. Paquin to the Northwoods. We gladly accepted, and began what was to be for both of us, but especially for me, a welcome friendship.

Mr. Paquin had lived much of his life in New York City, but on his retirement from the entertainment world had returned to Michigamme to stay with his aging mother. He had applied for a job as an extra in Anatomy, he told me, just out of nostalgia, to get back into the theater business for a brief moment, and had found that he thoroughly enjoyed it.

Mr. Paquin often invited me to his house for tea and cookies after that, keeping me hanging on his every word as he told me fascinating stories of the world of drama.

The first stage play he ever saw took place in the Ishpeming Theater, which was also a movie house and still existed as such during the filming of John Voelker's book. At the time Lawrence saw the play he was just thirteen years old, and he determined that day, as he left the theater, that he would seek a career in drama.

The star of that presentation, Mortimer Flynn, a famed Shakespearean actor, was a relative of my McCarthy family, and one of my "uncles" was named Edmund Mortimer Flynn.

Edmund, or Red as we called him because of his hair, was the first one of those whom the aunts had raised from an early age. He always went by Edmund Mortimer McCarthy until he entered the Navy during World War II and had to be known by his real name.

Lawrence Paquin saved the program from that introduction to theater. He subsequently went on to keep the stage bills from every play he saw throughout his life, and there were many.

We would spread a few of them on his table on each of my visits and read each one together as he made comments about the play or the actors. Many of the actors he had known personally, and could relate little anecdotes about them which were always interesting, and often humorous.

Lawrence made fun of himself in telling the story of the son of some friends, a boy whom he thought of as pretty much of a brat. But even brats grow up, and when the boy became a man he auditioned before Mr. Paquin for a part in one of Lawrence's productions on Broadway. Still thinking of the young man as the annoying child who had once plagued him, Lawrence did not cast him in the play. So the brat went out to Hollywood, hit it big, and became an almost instant star. Tyrone Power!

Lawrence was a very striking gentleman with thick and wavy white hair and a straight, graceful walk. And "gentleman" is a very appropriate description of his demeanor. Soft-spoken and always the picture of courtesy, he put his companions at ease at all times.

But neither was he a prude. He liked to tell the story of his one return to New York City after having retired, a trip undertaken with the intent of seeing the best of the current productions.

As a member of the Lamb's Club, a theatrical organization, he stayed at their clubhouse instead of a hotel. Since many of the theaters were within a few blocks of the club and he would be walking to and from the plays, he deposited his money with the desk clerk for safety purposes.

One night on his return stroll, a young, very red-headed woman (to use his words) came up to him.

"Hello, Sir," she said politely. "My, you have lovely hair."

Mr. Paquin smiled. "Why thank you, my dear. And so do you."

"It's too nice a night to be walking alone, don't you think?" she queried innocently, eyes wide. "Mind if I join you?"

"Not at all," was the answer as he tried to hide a chuckle, waiting to see what would come next.

He didn't have to wait long. As they approached a bar, she suggested, "Why don't we just stop in here and have a little drink?"

Not being much interested in alcohol, and not being at all interested in what obviously was to follow it, he told her, "I'm sorry, but I can't. For three reasons."

Her ingenuous smile hardened a bit as she resignedly asked, bored now, "What's the first one?"

"I haven't any money."

"You can take the other two and shove 'em!" she snapped, hurrying off down the street.

* * *

While Lawrence Paquin's name was not included in the credits, one local person's was. Lloyd LeVasseur had been the Marquette County clerk for a good many years when the filming began, and his duties included being present in the courtroom during trials. For this reason, he was selected to play himself. His is the voice we hear calling for order, and his is the gavel whose insistent announcement thuds over the crowd. One of John's pet peeves had always been movies in which the judge himself pounded the gavel to announce that court was in session. Perhaps this was acceptable in some areas, but not in Marquette County.

Cut! Prrrint!

After two months of shooting, "Anatomy of a Murder" was finished. Actors proceeded to other locations and other films, and the crew packed up all the equipment to return to Hollywood before proceeding to jobs on other productions. The excitement was over. Directors and musicians would put the final touches on the cutting and background music, and promotion of the movie, which had been taking place throughout the filming, would now begin in earnest.

Ishpeming would gradually return to normal, but it had been touched by a small bit of magic which would long be remembered by those who were there.

* * *

Much has changed since 1959 and all that excitement in our little town. And much has not.

The courthouse still reigns regally over Marquette, Michigan, and still retains many of the same physical attributes it had in 1959. It has had a few facelifts here and there, and a new wing has been added, but much of the old girl gazes down on us just as she did then. She changes her outside attire with the seasons, looking green and cheerful during the summer, glowing with reds, oranges and yellows in autumn, turning white and icy for our long winters, and in the spring taking on the dull brown visage that was hers as Anatomy was being committed to film to be enjoyed throughout all these intervening years.

Watching gently over Ishpeming, The Mather Inn still stands, but her voice is stilled. The music is gone. The flowers are gone. There are no laughing guests. It is quiet now. When the Inn was owned by the mining company, operating at a loss was of little importance. The hotel was a convenience for visiting dignitaries, salespeople, and company members from Cleveland. Such luminaries as Artur Rubinstein, Fritz Kreisler and many more graced the Inn with their presence when they visited Ishpeming to perform in the Al Quaal concert series in the Ishpeming High School auditorium. It is not to our credit, though, that when the contralto Marian Anderson gave us the pleasure of a performance it was suggested that she go to the Anderson Hotel, which usually housed the porters from the trains. Fortunately though, thanks to many local protests, the powers-that-be relented and she stayed at the Mather Inn. And, just as importantly, most of that old prejudice had disappeared by the time Duke Ellington arrived.

But under private ownership, operating at a loss does not fill the bill.

The Inn has gone through several new owners in the years that followed, opening for a while and then closing again. The gentleman who now owns it has been in the process of renovating the upper floors for several years. Eventually it will house apartments, but it has been a very slow process. For a while he had the Tap Room open, but apparently that didn't work out. It just wasn't the same as it had been in those long-ago days when The Mather Inn was the center of our social lives.

Mount Shasta has also gone through many owners but looks almost exactly as it did during the filming. Inside decorations and furniture have come and gone, but the huge old logs are still warmly enclosing their guests, and the parking lot has not changed, even to the half-circle cement steps leading from it to the dining room.

On a divider separating the bar area from the dining room are hung large framed photographs of many of those involved in the movie. John Voelker looks handsome and pensive as he gazes out a window. Eve Arden is seen sitting with Jimmy Stewart in his convertible eating lunch. There is a close-up of Kathryn Grant, as well as a shot of Lee Remick on the couch in one of the office scenes at the Voelker home. Otto Preminger is shown in the town of Michigamme with a background of old buildings, many of which are still standing. Arthur O'Connell also appears in Michigamme. There is a shot of Jimmy Stewart playing the piano with Duke Ellington at Mount Shasta, and one of him in the courtroom scene where we see Brooks West in the background. In another of the photos, Jimmy and Lee Remick are found standing outside the courthouse building with the dog, Muffy.

At the center of all these celebrities is a photo of the corpse portrayed by Robert Brebner of Marquette, a regular Mount Shasta customer and camper on one of the many smaller lakes in the area. This picture as well as two others of Bob are introduced as evidence in the courtroom scene.

The town of Michigamme has undergone some sprucing up in recent years, but it is still the same quiet, serene little village. Several shops have been opened offering gift items, art work and crafts, enticing summer tourists from U.S. 41 to buy or browse.

The huge old Gossard factory building which boasted the chiming clock of Duke Ellington's "Midnight Indigo" is now the Pioneer Mall, owned and run by the son of our next-door neighbors when we lived on the lake. It contains a variety of businesses and also the District Court. Sadly the clock is silent now, heard only in Edward Kennedy Ellington's notes.

Still standing on the corner of Main and Barnum Streets, Ishpeming's Carnegie Public Library looks, at least from the outside, exactly as it did when Jimmy Stewart leaned over the railing to quote the law to Arthur O'Connell. Not much has changed inside, either, although automation has struck.

What once was the Ishpeming Theater, the site of the Shakespearean play which introduced Lawrence Paquin to the Thespian arts, is now a parking lot for Paul Arsenault's Pioneer Mall.

The Congress Bar and Pizza still opens its doors to Main Street just across from the statue of Old Ish. This the bar where we first meet Arthur O'Connell in the movie.

And Kathryn Grant Crosby would be happy to know that Donckers Candies & Gifts is still satisfying the sweet-tooths of Marquette County and many other areas.

The Northland Hotel reopened several years ago after being closed for a long time, and the new owner has kept its former charm and beauty, even though much of it had to be restored. It has been renamed The Landmark Inn, with the bar bearing the title The Northland Bar.

Some things change around here, but happily not too much. We, as did John D. Voelker, like it as it is.

"Anatomy of a Murder" was nominated for seven Academy Awards, including best picture. James Stewart received a nomination for best actor, Arthur O'Connell and George C. Scott for best supporting actors, Sam Leavitt again for black and white cinematography, Louis Loeffler for film editing, and Wendell Mayes for screenwriter of a play based on material from another medium.

In April of 1989, the John D. Voelker Foundation was founded. It not only honors its namesake but also grants scholarships to deserving students who are pursuing law degrees, preferably, if possible, to Native Americans. The first recipient was George W. Hyde III, a member of the Sault Ste. Marie Chippewa Tribe, who received his award in 1991 while attending Cooley Law School in Lansing, Michigan. He had earned his undergraduate degree from Northern Michigan University in Marquette, which was also John Voelker's undergraduate alma mater and, I'm proud to say, my own. According to "Tin Cup Times," newsletter of the John D. Voelker Foundation, Mr. Hyde graduated cum laude in the top ten percent of his class on January 15, 1994, from Cooley Law School. It would appear the board made a good choice. On September 14, 1996, Mr. Hyde was elected to the Voelker Foundation Board of Directors.

In conjunction with the magazine, "Fly Rod & Reel," an annual John D. Voelker Fly Fishing Fiction Award is bestowed upon some deserving writer.

President of the Voelker foundation is Richard F. Vander Veen III, a great admirer of John and a sometime fishing partner in days past. Serving as vice president is James F. Graves, and as secretary-treasurer Frederick M. Baker, Jr. On the board of directors is another fishing and cribbage partner and old friend, Anthony "Gigs" Gagliardi. Also on the board are two of John's daughters, Grace Voelker Wood (Gracie) and Julie Voelker Cohen, and two of his grandsons, Adam J. Tsaloff, Honey-Bee's son, and John Voelker Overturf, Julie's son. John W. Cummiskey, Nick Lyons, John Frey, Walter Abbot, and George Hyde, the first recipient of the Voelker award, complete the board at the time of this writing.

Deceased members of the Voelker Foundation board of directors are John D. Voelker (1903-1991) and the well-known television personality, Charles Kuralt (1934-1997).

Charles Kuralt and John were good friends. Mr. Kuralt featured John in one of his CBS "On the Road" television shows, and fished with the author on John's beloved Frenchman's Pond in the Upper Peninsula. Mr. Kuralt was instrumental in getting newscaster Tom Brokaw to join also.

Another well-known member is the film actor Jeff Daniels, whose home is in Lower Michigan. Jeff has ties to Marquette, as his wife's parents used to live here. We were their friends, having met them during our active years in the now extinct Marquette Community Theater.

Recently the Foundation logo was redesigned, depicting the three main aspects of John's life -- the law, writing and fishing. A scale represents the law, a book depicts John's writing, and a fish shows his hobby. This idea was conceived by Joanne Gagliardi, whose husband, Gigs, is a member of the board of directors of the Foundation. The design was created at Globe Printing, Inc. under a work-study program. A student, Trevor Nicholas, designed the logo with the supervision of Stacey Willey, Globe Printing's Production Manager and now its long-time owner..

Over fifty years have passed since Boris Leven and Henry Weinberger sat at a table in the Georgian Room of the Mather Inn and discussed the sites which would become part of "Anatomy of a Murder." It is a long time since the dining room burst with movie shop talk and the voices and laughter of guests there to watch and admire; a long time since cars lined up on East Barnum Street in the early morning hours to load their actors and crew and carry them to the site of the day; a long time since romances bloomed, irritations surfaced, and friendships grew. So much has changed in regard to the people who were involved back in 1959. Many are dead -- James Stewart, Arthur O'Connell, Duke Ellington, Murray Hamilton, Billy Strayhorn, Lee Remick, Colleen Dewhurst and Mr. Preminger among them. And of course Ishpeming will always miss John Voelker, one of its most be-loved and most loyal citizens.

John died in his car of a heart attack on March 18, 1991 at the age of eighty-seven. He just went off the road, hurting no one, and fell asleep. A sad event for all of us who had known and loved him.

John never did give up that much-enjoyed old pastime of playing cribbage at the Wonder Bar when he couldn't fish or wasn't writing. I'm sure the game was happily accompanied by his well-known "bour-bon out of an old tin cup," though the cup may have been a bar glass and not made of tin.

My favorite and just about only place to shop for clothes in those years was The Style Shop, also now long gone. The Style Shop was a lovely women's store which had been a landmark in Ishpeming since the early nineteen hundreds. It was on Main Street but had a side side door around the corner and just across the street from the Wonder Bar. Many are the times, as I parked by that side door on Pearl Street, when John would lean out the door of the Wonder Bar, wave gracefully at me (John's movements were always serene and graceful), and shout in that easy, unhurried way of his, "Hi, Joanie! How's Barnum Street?" This, though neither of us had lived there for years.

I can see him now. And hear him. And miss him.

Testament Of A Fisherman

I fish because I love to; because I love the environs where trout are found, which are invariably beautiful, and hate the environs where crowds of people are found, which are invariably ugly; because of all the television commercials, cocktail parties, and assorted social posturing I thus escape; because in a world where most men seem to spend their lives doing things they hate, my fishing is at once an endless source of delight and an act of small rebellion; because trout do not lie or cheat and cannot be bought or bribed or impressed by power, but respond only to quietude and humility and endless patience; because I suspect that men are going along this way for the last time, and I for one don't want to waste the trip; because mercifully there are no telephones on trout waters; because only in the woods can I find solitude without loneliness; because bourbon out of an old tin cup always tastes better out there; because maybe one day I will catch a mermaid; and finally, not because I regard fishing as being so terribly important but because I suspect that so many of the other concerns of men are equally unimportant — and not nearly so much fun.

John Voelker
(Robert Traver)

"I fish because I love to; because I love the environs where trout are found, which are invariably beautiful, and hate the environs where crowds of people are found, which are invariably ugly; . . . because only in the woods can I find solitude without loneliness; because bourbon out of an old tin cup always tastes better out there; . . ."

From "Testament of a Fisherman" by Robert Traver (John D. Voelker) Reprinted with permission of Grace T. Voelker.

Feb. 12, 1988

Dear Joanie,
As soon as I can get
my player friend will play
your tape. I will look
forward to the prospect
and meanwhile thank you
for remembering those old
inhabitants of Iron Lane:
residences of old West Barnum street,
^ please
that used to read like a
^ map of Dublin, begorrah!
          Best to you both.
                    John

Ishpeming / Aug. 25,
                    1980

Dear Joanie,
          It missed my adoption
by Marquette, and join Barnum
Street in fighting this base
canard.
          Thanks & best to you
and Walter.
                    John

Ishpeming / Jan. 14, 1981

Dear Joanie,
          I both loved and learned
a lot from your piece on Beaver
Island -- where I've never been,
but mean to mend my ways.

          Mary Clancy also sent me
a photo-copy of a letter from
three sisters with a running
commentary of the residences of
^ road- map of old West Barnum
street, but forgot to tell me who
they were. Can you fill me in?

          Your piece is delightful,
and do keep it up. And thank
you so much for sending it to
me.
          Best to you both,
                    John

ONE ADMISSION TO

WORLD SPECIAL PREVIEW

First Public Showing Of
OTTO PREMINGER'S

FROM THE NOVEL BY

JOHN D. VOELKER (Robert Traver)
Michigan Supreme Court Justice
and Native Son of the Upper Peninsula

BUTLER THEATRE
ISHPEMING, MICH.

Admission ....$ 1.00
Bay Cliff Donation 9.00

Total $10.00

MONDAY EVENING — 7:30

JUNE 29

NINETEEN HUNDRED AND FIFTY-NINE

ALL PROCEEDS DONATED TO

BAY CLIFF HEALTH CAMP

Program Cover

The motion picture you are about to see could not have been filmed without the inspiration of one of your fellow citizens, Justice John D. Voelker, or without the wonderful cooperation of the people of Marquette County. I think it only fitting, then, that you and he should be the first to view "Anatomy of a Murder."

—Otto Preminger,
Producer-Director

JAMES STEWART

LEE REMICK

EVE ARDEN

KATHRYN GRANT

JOSEPH N. WELCH

ARTHUR O'CONNELL

BEN GAZZARA

DUKE ELLINGTON

Above is an inside page of the Premier "Anatomy of a Murder" Program. The original program was printed at Globe Printing in Ishpeming, MI for the 1959 World Special Preview at the Butler Theater. Reprinted with permission of Globe Printing.

Marquette County Court House

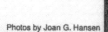
Photos by Joan G. Hansen

Front Entrance

Side Entrance
Near the Jail

Marble Stairway
and Stained Glass
Windows

Photos by Joan G. Hansen

The Main
Courtroom

Carnegie Public Library

Corner of Barnum and Main

Photo by Joan G. Hansen

The Mather Inn

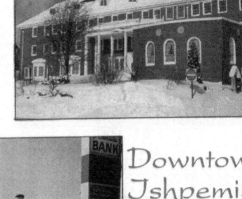

Downtown Ishpeming Michigan

Main Street

Photos by Joan G. Hansen

"Old Ish" and The Peninsula Bank

John D. Voelker

IHS annual 1922

"Handsome John"
1922 Ishpeming High
School Graduation

John in 1991, at one of
his Favorite Games of
Cribbage

Photo reprinted from Ishpeming High School's "Beacon Light"

West Barnum Street

Photos by Joan G. Hansen

The John Voelker
Home, Corner of
Barnum and Pine

Mt. Shasta

Photos by Joan G. Hansen

Photos of Some of the Cast and Crew

The Signature Wall at The Roosevelt Night Club

(Now Globe Printing, Inc.)

Photos by Daniel T. Willey

Made in the USA
Lexington, KY
03 November 2019